EMPOWERED
FOR
FREEDOM

INNER HEALING AND DELIVERANCE MANUAL

TEIA MARTINEZ

MINISTRIES

EMPOWERED FOR FREEDOM INNER: HEALING AND DELIVERANCE MANUAL

For information about this title or to order other books and/or electronic media, contact the publisher:

Teia Martinez

Publisher email: office@teiamartinezministries.com

Printed in the United States of America

ISBN: 979-8-9937163-0-5

DEDICATION

I dedicate this manual to the Lord, for He is the one who has given me purpose in my life, and the tools for healing. My prayer is that He would multiply and bless many through it .

FOREWORD

Around 20 years ago, my friends Dr. Bill and Janet Sudduth introduced me to their ministry team, which included Teia Martinez. They taught her well, and our regular connecting through the annual conferences of the International Society of Deliverance Ministers have kept us in touch personally through the years.

One of the greatest joys of ministry is to see younger people grow and mature and that is certainly true of Teia. I am thrilled to see her new book, Empowered for Freedom, which provides the tools for many to be set free from those bondages that hold people back from spiritual, physical and emotional healing and wholeness. Teia's book is DIY (Do It Yourself) as it's easy to understand and apply. I'm sure this book will be used widely to those purposes, and I know Bill and Janet would also be thrilled that Teia has produced this tool for freedom. I highly commend Teia Martinez and her book, Empowered for Freedom.

Selwyn R. Stevens, Ph.D.

President: Jubilee Resources International Inc.

Member: Apostolic Roundtable International Society of Deliverance Ministers

TABLE OF CONTENTS

ACKNOWLEDGMENTS

I want to thank my spiritual parents, **Bill and Janet Sudduth**, for always believing in me and equipping me with the tools and knowledge I've used in Inner Healing and Deliverance. They both continually pointed me to the Lord and modeled what it looks like to run the race with faith and perseverance. They are both with Jesus now, and I miss them deeply.

I also want to honor **Sylvie Sudduth**, who has faithfully continued his legacy and carried the torch of the ministry.

To my precious family — thank you for the sacrifices you've made while I've spent countless hours serving others and pursuing the Lord's call on my life. Your constant encouragement and cheering me on have been a gift beyond words.

To every volunteer who has served with Teia Martinez Ministries in so many different ways — from ministering alongside me to handling the behind-the-scenes work — I am deeply grateful. A special thank you to **Sara Michalski** and many others who have given your time, talents, and hearts to run with me in this vision.

I could not have gotten this far without the people God has placed in my life to stand with me, pray with me, and move forward together in His Kingdom work.

UNDERSTANDING INNER HEALING AND DELIVERANCE

What Is Inner Healing?

Inner healing is a personal encounter with Jesus, where He brings healing to the deep places in our hearts that have been wounded or broken.

It helps us deal with trauma, lies we've believed about ourselves or God, and the roots of emotional pain that can show up as anxiety, depression, fear, insecurity, or destructive patterns. Often, emotional struggles are tied to a specific moment in our story—a memory, a wound, a belief we picked up in childhood or through life experiences. Inner healing helps us go to that place with Jesus, let Him speak truth, and heal what's been hurting.

When the root is healed, the fruit can change. That's why this type of prayer ministry leads to real, lasting transformation—not just behavior management, but true freedom in the soul.

What Is Deliverance?

Deliverance is the process of breaking spiritual bondage and commanding evil spirits to leave in the name of Jesus.

When someone opens the door to sin, trauma, or occult activity—or when there's generational bondage in their bloodline—demons can gain access to torment or influence them. Deliverance ministry is not about fear or drama—it's about using the authority Jesus gave us to shut those doors, renounce what we've agreed with, and cast out whatever doesn't belong.

This is done in love, with dignity, and with the power of the Holy Spirit.

Deliverance and inner healing work hand in hand. Often, healing the wounds in a person's soul removes the foothold the enemy used to stay. That's why this manual includes tools for both—because true freedom comes when we heal the soul, cast out the enemy, and renew the mind with truth.

INTRODUCTION

Welcome to your ministry manual for healing and freedom.

This book was created to equip you with the tools, language, and spiritual authority needed to walk in—and minister—deep inner healing and lasting deliverance. Whether you're ministering to someone else or navigating your own personal breakthrough, this manual serves as a practical and Spirit-led guide to help you partner with God to bring freedom.

Inside, you'll find four key sections, each intentionally laid out to flow with the rhythm of a typical session—but also flexible enough to meet you right where you are.

Prayer Tools

These are ready-to-use, strategic prayers written to target specific issues clients may be struggling with, like shame, rejection, fear, or trauma. They're designed to be spoken aloud—either on your own, or for the client to repeat after the minister—to break agreement with lies, receive truth, and usher in the healing power of Jesus. These are placed in the front for quick access during sessions, but many link directly to teachings found later in the manual. We recommend reading the related Teaching Tools beforehand for deeper understanding and effectiveness.

Deliverance

This section gives you lists of common manifestations and fruit tied to specific strongholds—so clients can renounce what they're ready to release, and you can command those spirits to leave in Jesus' name. It also includes setup and closing prayers to help you anchor each session in peace and power.

Teaching Tools

Here's where we go deeper. This section offers you biblical and practical instruction on how to teach vital healing concepts like soul ties, generational patterns, or emotional wounds. It also includes guidance for ministering inner healing, and how to adapt to specific situations, such as post-abortion healing. These are foundational for helping the client to understand why they are praying what they are praying, and we recommend you familiarize yourself with this section to fully activate the power of the prayer tools.

Resources

This final section includes the forms and follow-up tools you'll need for real-world ministry: client questionnaires (for adults, teens, and children), consent forms (for adults and minors), and post-session guidance. These help you steward your sessions with wisdom, integrity, and care.

This manual is a complete equipping framework to minister healing and deliverance with clarity, compassion, and spiritual authority. Use it as a companion in your one-on-one sessions, your prayer closet, or your training of future leaders.

Whether you're stepping into this for the first time or have years of experience, our prayer is that this tool will equip you to grow in discernment, confidence, and sensitivity to the Holy Spirit.

You're not just reading a book. You're stepping into a move of God—and He has chosen **you** to be a vessel of His healing power.

Let's begin.

PART ONE:

PRAYER TOOLS

SPIRITUAL "Bolt-Cutter" PRAYER

Dear Heavenly Father:

I come to You in the name of the Lord Jesus Christ. And I renounce and turn from all lies, all preconceptions, deceptions, and self-deceptions, and all unteachableness that I or my ancestors have believed or entertained.

I confess them as my sins and I ask to be cleansed from them by the Blood of the Lord Jesus Christ. I renounce all vows of secrecy and silence about all ungodly activities.

I command every lying spirit, and every spirit of deception, self-deception, and unteachableness, and any other spirits associated with these sins to leave me now, harmlessly on my natural breathing, and not to return to me or to anyone whom I love, in the Name of the Lord Jesus Christ.

In the name of the Lord Jesus Christ, I come out of agreement with and renounce all shame, blame and guilt, all fear, all fear of failure, all fear of rejection, all fear of men, all fear of offending and ridicule, and all fear of not hearing God. Lord Jesus, you are the Truth, and I surrender all these areas to Your Holy Spirit, Who is the Spirit of Truth, and whom You promised would lead me into all truth. In Jesus' Name. Amen.

Written by Selwyn Stevens (JubileeResources.org)

This prayer helps take down defenses and deal with any fear before the session begins.

CATHOLICISM PRAYER

If you were once a member of the Roman Catholic Church or are a descendant of someone who was, we recommend that you pray through this prayer from your heart. Please read it through first so you know what is involved. It is best to pray this aloud with a mature Christian present. We suggest a brief pause following each paragraph to allow the Holy Spirit to show any related issues that may require attention.

Father God, creator of Heaven and Earth, I come to you in the name of the Lord Jesus Christ, your Son, my Savior. I come as a sinner seeking forgiveness and cleansing from all my sins committed against you. I honor my earthly father and mother, and all of my ancestors of flesh and blood, and of the spirit by adoption, and godparents, but I utterly turn away from and renounce all of their sins. I forgive all of my ancestors for the effects of their sins and iniquities on me and my descendants. I confess and renounce all of my own sins, known or unknown. I renounce and rebuke Satan and every spiritual power of his that affects me and my family in the name of Jesus Christ.

In the name of Jesus, I renounce and forsake all involvement in Roman Catholicism by myself and my ancestors. I renounce every covenant, every blood covenant, and every alliance with Roman Catholicism or the spiritual powers behind it made by me or my family. I also renounce and repent of all permission I have ever granted to be deceived, or that was granted by my parents or previous generations without my awareness or consent. I renounce every covenant made with death and hell.

I renounce and I repent for submitting to all ungodly authority and powers. I repent for my loyalty to the Roman Catholic Church, the Vatican, its Popes, Cardinals, Archbishops, Bishops, and Priests, when that loyalty and obedience should have been given to Jesus Christ alone. I also repent of and renounce any and all impartations or religious deception that I received through any laying on of hands by any false priesthood. I especially reject the false teaching and belief in the infallibility of the pope.

I repent for my ignorance and silence about the Roman Catholic Church's historical use of terror, bloodshed, torture, lies, coercion, deception, sexual immorality, fraud, control, and manipulation, done directly or through the various Orders of the Church. Please heal me from any of these things that have been done to me, or what was done to others, with or without my awareness or consent.

In the name of the Lord Jesus Christ, I repent for believing in a church that has kept people from understanding the Holy Bible, the written Word of God. I humbly ask to be exempted from the punishment in Revelation 22:18-19 for adding or subtracting from God's Word.

I renounce all syncretism and paganism taught alongside true Biblical teaching by the Roman Catholic Church. I reject, renounce, and repent of all pagan beliefs and practices, and I ask to be set free from all pagan influences in my mind, my will, my emotions, my heart, my conscience, my imagination, and my habits.

I choose to forgive and ask for mercy for everyone who has taught me and others false doctrines, ungodly religious practices, including the so-called "Sacrifice of the Mass." I also renounce and reject the calling on the spirits of the dead to protect me that occurs at every mass.

In the name of the Lord Jesus Christ, I renounce and repent of every form of idolatry, including the idolatry of the quote, "Holy Mother Church," and any false worship and spiritual adultery I have been involved in.

In the name of the Lord Jesus Christ, I repent of and renounce every devotion, veneration, and all worship and idolatry of the Virgin Mary. I renounce the unbiblical belief in Mary's omniscience. I also reject and renounce the falsely claimed Co-Mediatory and Intercessory roles of Mary, the title "Mother of God," the Immaculate Conception, Co-Redemptrix, her Perpetual Virginity (despite having at least six other named children), and her Bodily Assumption into Heaven.

I also renounce the belief in the post-death apparitions of Mary, such as the Lady of Lourdes, Lady of Fatima, Lady of Guadeloupe, and all others. I reject all instruction from these and all other similar apparitions because too many of those instructions were contrary to the revealed Word of God. I also reject and renounce all other titles given to Mary, including Mother of God, Queen of Heaven, Lady of Mercedes, Lady of the Snows, Queen of Martyrs, Queen of Peace, Star of the Seas, Black Madonna, and any other titles attributed to her.

In the name of the Lord Jesus Christ, I repent and ask your forgiveness for praying to dead people and dead saints, and the necromancy and spiritism involved, which the Holy Bible clearly forbids in Deuteronomy 18:11 and elsewhere.

I repent, renounce, and break all ungodly soul ties and connections and all dedication of my life to dead saints, including Mary, and also any dedication to any organization, including the Roman Catholic Church. In cancelling that now, I choose to dedicate my life to the Lord Jesus Christ.

In the name of the Lord Jesus Christ, I repent of and renounce all trust in dedicated objects, including medals, scapulars, statues, sacred heart posters and paintings, rosary beads, holy water, votive candles, sacred relics, and any kissing or bowing to any alleged sacred object or novena. I also repent for trusting in rituals and objects and attributing power to them instead of trusting and relying on Your love, power, and faithfulness.

I also repent, and renounce all trust in any "sacrament" that does not have a solid Biblical basis, including infant baptism, confirmation, first communion or Eucharist, confession, penance, and extreme unction. I renounce the unbiblical belief in the continual sacrifice of Jesus on the cross during communion, and I confess that He was sacrificed for all as a perfect and complete sacrifice.

I renounce all beliefs that are contrary to the written Word and will of God, and I ask for You to renew my mind and my heart, and help me recognize all false teaching and beliefs when I hear or see them. Please protect me from all spiritual deception, regardless of its source, in Jesus' name.

I reject and renounce the shameless fraud called indulgences, used to obtain money from members of the Roman Catholic Church by priests, with false and unsubstantiated promises of quicker release from the imaginary place of the dead called Purgatory, or of the falsely promised cancellation of sins.

I reject, repent of, and renounce every form of sexual immorality; all perversion, pedophilia, seduction, rape, the killing of babies, and the hypocrisy involved in the Roman Catholic Church by priests and clergy. I also reject the enforced celibacy of clergy, priests, and nuns.

I repent of serving a church that required people to fast through legalism, and that killed people for eating meat during Lent.

Please enable me to recognize all error and false teaching. I especially renounce and repent of ever believing the anti-Biblical teachings of transubstantiation, purgatory, and that my salvation may only be obtained by being baptized into membership of the Roman Catholic Church as an infant. I recognize that the elements of communion are only symbolic of the body and blood of Jesus Christ.

I renounce and rebuke every evil spirit associated with Roman Catholicism, spiritism, occultic mysticism, and all other sins and iniquities involved. Lord Jesus, I ask you to now set me free from all spiritual and other bondages, in accordance with the many promises of the Bible. In the name of the Lord Jesus Christ, I now bind and break every spirit of sickness, infirmity, every curse, including the curse of Trent. Every affliction, addiction, disease, or allergy associated with these sins I have confessed and renounced, including every spirit empowering all iniquities inherited from my family.

Holy Spirit, I ask that you show me anything else that I need to do or to pray so that I and my family may be totally free from the consequences of the sins of Roman Catholicism, witchcraft, spiritism, and all related paganism and occultism.

(Pause, listen to God, and pray as the Holy Spirit leads you.)

Now, dear Father God, I ask humbly for the blood of Jesus Christ to cleanse me from all these sins I have confessed and renounced, to cleanse my spirit, my soul, my mind, will and emotions, and every part of my body which has been affected by these sins, in the name of Jesus Christ. I also command every cell in my body to come into divine order now, and to be healed and made whole as they were designed to by my loving Creator, including restoring all chemical imbalances and neurological functions, controlling all cancerous cells, reversing all degenerative diseases, and severing the DNA and RNA of any mental or physical diseases or afflictions that came down through my family bloodlines.

I ask you, Lord, to fill me with your Holy Spirit now, according to the promises in your Word. I take to myself the whole armor of God in accordance with Ephesians chapter six, and I rejoice in its protection as Jesus surrounds me and fills me with His Holy Spirit. I enthrone you, Lord Jesus, in my heart, for you are my Lord and my Savior, the source of eternal life. Thank you, Father God, for Your mercy, Your forgiveness, and Your love.

I command every evil spirit to leave me now, touching or harming no one, and go to a dry and arid place, never to return to me or my family. In Jesus' name! Amen.

Modified version of prayer from Rome's Anathemas: Insights into the Papal Pantheon, ISBN 978-1-87746389-1 by Selwyn R. Stevens (JubileeResources.org)

COVID PRAYER

Heavenly Father, I come to You for healing and freedom. I come against every virus, in particular Covid. The Spirit that raised Jesus from the dead is living in me, and You promised He would also give life to my mortal body. (Rom 8:11)

I repent of and renounce all spirits of fear and death that came in through sickness, through psychological warfare, through news stations, social media, what family members or spiritual leaders may have spoken in fear, or pressure from society. I renounce all fear, especially during the night. I renounce the fear of getting sick or getting someone else sick. I renounce the fear of dying, of my lungs shutting down, of not being able to breathe. I renounce the fear of family or loved ones dying. I renounce spiritual death or death of my desire to go to church or meet with other believers. I renounce the collapse of my will that would have me give up and give in to the spirit of death. I break the power of fear and death over my life right now, in the powerful name of Jesus.

I renounce all symptoms I experienced with Covid, including high fever, night sweats, diarrhea, vomiting, the sensation of brain frying or burning headache, chest pain, chest heaviness, sinus infections, blood clots in lungs or body, and body aches. (Add any other symptoms you experienced that are not listed.) I renounce any power that Covid has to bring death between 3 and 5 AM. I renounce the spirit of infirmity that can come with long haul symptoms. I break the power of every effect of Covid on my physical body right now, and I receive the truth that by Jesus' stripes, I AM healed.

I repent for agreeing with all fear or control-driven agendas related to Covid. I renounce psychological warfare in every form. I renounce false information and witchcraft. I renounce any control over my mind, body, or God-given rights that I have yielded because of fear or witchcraft. I renounce the spirit of antichrist that comes against the true Word and Move of God. I will not submit to any ungodly agenda, plan, or structure, I submit only to the Holy Spirit, and to His plans for me. I renounce any fear of seeing or knowing the truth. I break the power of all mind control, all slumber, and all enchantment. I remove any veil that was placed over my eyes to keep me from seeing the truth, and I ask you Lord to open my spiritual eyes and ears, to anything You want me to see or hear.

I declare over myself, that I am more than a conqueror through Him who loves me, and that neither death nor life, neither angels nor demons, neither the present nor the future, nor any powers, neither height nor depth, nor anything else in all creation will be able to separate me from the love of God that is in Christ Jesus our Lord. (Romans 8:37-39)

God will restore me to health and heal my wounds. (Jeremiah 30:17)

Jesus Himself bore my sins in His body on the cross, so that I might die to sins and live for righteousness; by His wounds I have been healed. (1 Peter 2:24)

I will not allow my heart to be troubled, and I will not be afraid. Jesus has given me His peace. (John 14:27)

God gives strength to the weary and increases the power of the weak, so I receive His strength and power. (Isaiah 40:29)

The righteous (I belong to and trust in Jesus as my Savior, so that's me) cry out, and the Lord hears me; He delivers me from all my troubles. The Lord is close to the brokenhearted and saves those who are crushed in spirit. The righteous person (that's me) may have many troubles, but the Lord delivers me from them all; He protects all my bones, not one of them will be broken. Evil will slay the wicked; the foes of the righteous will be condemned. The Lord will rescue me; no one who takes refuge in Him will be condemned. I choose to take refuge in the Lord! (Psalm 34:17-22)

Lord, I receive your healing, your strength, and your freedom in my body and soul. I bless my body with Divine health, from the top of my head to the bottom of my feet. I command every function in my body to come into alignment with the truth of the Word of God. I choose to stand on Your truth until I see it fully manifest in my body, and I receive full healing from any remaining symptoms of Covid. I give You all the praise and glory for my total healing. In the powerful name of Jesus, Amen.

FREEMASONRY PRAYER

If you were once a Mason or are a descendant of a Mason, we recommend that you pray through the following prayer from your heart. Do not be like the Masons who are given their obligations and oaths one line at a time and without prior knowledge of the requirements. Please read it through first so you know what is involved. It is best to pray this aloud with a Christian witness or counselor present. We suggest a brief pause following each paragraph to allow the Holy Spirit to show any additional issues which may require attention: However, I prefer to read this prayer to them and have them repeat it after.

Father God, creator of heaven and earth, I come to You in the name of Jesus Christ, Your Son. I come as a sinner seeking forgiveness and cleansing from all sins committed against You. I honor my earthly father and mother and all of my ancestors of flesh and blood, and of the spirit by adoption and godparents, but I utterly turn away from and renounce all their sins. I forgive all my ancestors for the effects of their sins on me and my children. I confess and renounce all of my own sins. I renounce and rebuke Satan and every spiritual power of his affecting me and my family.

I renounce and forsake all involvement in Freemasonry or any other lodge or craft by my ancestors and myself. I renounce witchcraft, the principal spirit behind Freemasonry, and I renounce Baphomet, the spirit of Antichrist and the curse of the Luciferian doctrine. I renounce the idolatry, blasphemy, secrecy and deception of Masonry at every level. I specifically renounce the insecurity, the love of position and power, the love of money, avarice or greed, and the pride which would have led my ancestors into Masonry. I renounce all the fears, which held them in Masonry, especially the fears of death, fears of men, and fears of trusting. In Jesus' name, Amen.

I renounce every position held in the lodge by any of my ancestors, including "Tyler," "Master," "Worshipful Master," or any other. I renounce the calling of any man "Master," for Jesus Christ is my only master and Lord, and He forbids anyone else having that title. I renounce the entrapping of others into Masonry, and observing the helplessness of others during the rituals. I renounce the effects of Masonry passed on to me through any female ancestor who felt distrusted and rejected by her husband as he entered and attended any lodge and refused to tell her of his secret activities, in Jesus' name.

1st Degree I renounce the oaths taken and curses involved in the First or entered Apprentice degree, especially their effects on the throat and tongue. I renounce the Hoodwink, the blindfold, and its effects on emotions and eyes, including all confusion, fear of the dark, fear of the light, and fear of sudden noises. I renounce the secret word, BOAZ, and all it means. I renounce the mixing and mingling of truth and error, and the blasphemy of this degree of Masonry. I renounce the noose around the neck, the fear of choking and also every spirit causing asthma, hay fever, allergies, emphysema or any other breathing difficulty. I renounce the compass point, sword or spear held against the breast, the fear of death by stabbing pain, and the fear of heart attack from this degree. In the name of Jesus Christ, I now pray for healing of …(the throat, vocal cords, nasal passages, sinus, bronchial tubes and for healing of the speech area, and the release of the Word of God to me and through me, and my family. In Jesus' name, Amen.

2nd Degree I renounce the oaths taken and the curses involved in the second or Fellow Craft degree of Masonry, especially the curses on the heart, chest and lung area. I renounce the secret words JACHIN and SHIBBOLETH and all that these mean. I cut off all emotional hardness, apathy, indifference, unbelief, and deep anger from me and my family.

In the name of Jesus Christ, I now pray for the healing of…. (The chest/lung/heart area) and also for the healing of my emotions, and ask to be made sensitive to the Holy Spirit of God. In Jesus' name, Amen.

3rd Degree I renounce the oaths taken and the curses involved in the third or Master mason degree, especially the curses on the stomach and womb area. I renounce the secret words MAHABONE, MACHABEN, MACHBINNA and TUBAL CAIN, and all that they mean. I renounce the spirit of Death from the blows to the head enacted as ritual murder, the fear of death, false martyrdom, fear of violent gang attack, assault, or rape, and the helplessness of this degree. I renounce the falling into a coffin or stretcher involved in the ritual of murder. I renounce the false resurrection of this degree, because only Jesus Christ is the Resurrection and the Life! I also renounce the blasphemous kissing of the Bible on a Witchcraft oath. I cut off all spirits of death, witchcraft and deception and in the name of Jesus Christ I now pray for healing of …. (The stomach, gall bladder, womb, liver, and any other organs of my body affected by Masonry), and I ask for a release of compassion and understanding for me and my family. In Jesus' name, Amen.

York Rite Degree I renounce and forsake the oaths taken and the curses involved in the York Rite degrees of Masonry. I renounce the Mark Lodge, and the mark in the form of squares and angles which marks the person for life. I also reject the jewel or talisman which may have been made from this mark and worn at lodge meetings. I renounce the Mark Master Degree with its secret word JOPPA, and its penalty of having the right ear smote off and the curse of permanent deafness, as well as the right hand being chopped off for being an impostor. In Jesus' name, Amen.

I also renounce and forsake the oaths taken and the curses involved in the other York Rite Degrees, including Past Master, with the penalty of having my tongue split from tip to root.

I also renounce and forsake the oaths taken and the curses involved in the Most Excellent Master Degree, in which the penalty is to have my breast torn open and my heart and vital organs removed and exposed to rot on the dung hill. In Jesus' name, Amen.

Holy Royal Arch Degree I renounce and forsake the oaths taken and the curses involved in the Holy Royal Arch Degree of Masonry, especially the oath regarding the removal of the head from the body and the exposing of the brains to the hot sun. I renounce the false secret name of God JAHBULON, and the secret password AMMI RUHAMAH and all they mean. I renounce the false communion or Eucharist taken in this degree, I renounce all the mockery, skepticism and unbelief about the redemptive work of Jesus Christ on the cross of Calvary. I cut off all these curses and their effects on me and my family in the name of Jesus Christ, and now I pray for healing of…(the brain, and the mind.) In Jesus' name, Amen.

I renounce and forsake the oaths taken and the curses involved in the Royal Master Degree of the York Rite and the Select Master Degree with its penalty to have my hands chopped off to the stumps, to have my eyes plucked out from their sockets and to have my body quartered and thrown among the rubbish of the Temple. In Jesus' name, Amen.

I renounce and forsake the oaths taken and the curses involved in the Super Excellent Master Degree along with the penalty of having my thumbs cut off, my eyes put out, my body bound in fetters of brass, and conveyed captive to a strange land; and I also renounce the Knights Order of the Red Cross, along with the penalty of having my house torn down and my being hanged on the exposed timbers. In Jesus' name, Amen.

I renounce the other secret words of KEB RAIOTH and MAHER-SHALAL-HASH-BAZ. and all that they mean. I renounce the vows taken on a human skull, the crossed swords, and the curse and death wish of Judas, and of having the head cut off and placed on top of a church spire. I renounce the unholy communion and especially of drinking from a human skull in many rites. In Jesus' name, Amen.

18th Degree I renounce and forsake the oaths taken and the curses involved in the eighteenth degree of Masonry, and the Most Wise Sovereign Knight of the Pelican and the Eagle and Sovereign Prince Rose Croix of Heredom. I renounce and reject the Pelican witchcraft spirit, as well as the occultic influence of the Rosicrucians and the Kabala in this degree. I renounce the claim that the death of Jesus Christ was a "dire calamity" and also the deliberate mockery and twisting of the Christian doctrine of the Atonement. I renounce the blasphemy and rejection of the deity of Jesus Christ, and the secret words IGNE NATURA RENOVATUR INTEGRA and its meaning. I renounce the mockery of the communion taken in this degree, including a biscuit, salt and white wine. In Jesus' name, Amen.

I renounce the oaths taken and the curses involved in the American and Grand Orient Lodges, including the Secret Master Degree and its secret password ADONAI used blasphemously and its penalties.

I renounce the oaths taken and the curses involved in the Perfect Master Degree. its secret password MAH-HAH-BONE, and its penalty of being smitten to the Earth with a setting maul.

I renounce the oaths taken and the curses involved in the Intimate Secretary Degree, its secret password JEHOVAH used blasphemously, and its penalties of having my body dissected, and of having my vital organs cut into pieces and thrown to the beasts of the field.

I renounce the oaths taken and the curses involved in the Provost and Judge Degree, its secret password HIRUM-TITO-CIVI-KY and the penalty of having my nose cut off.

I renounce the oaths taken and the curses involved in the Intendant of the Building Degree, its secret password AKAR-JAI-JAH, and the penalty of having my eyes put out, my body cut in two and exposing my bowels.

I renounce the oaths taken and the curses involved in the Elected Knights of the ninth degree, its secret password NEKAM NAKAH, and its penalty of having my head cut off and stuck on the highest pole in the East.

I renounce the oaths taken and the curses involved in the Illustrious Elect of Fifteenth Degree with its secret password ELIGNAM, and its penalties of having my body opened perpendicularly and horizontally, and entrails exposed to the air for eight hours so that flies may prey on them, and for my head to be cut off and placed on a high pinnacle.

I renounce the oaths taken and the curses involved in the Sublime Knights elect of the twelfth Degree, its secret password STOLKIN-ADONAI, and its penalty of having my hand cut in twain.

I renounce the oaths taken and the curses involved in the Grand Master Architect Degree, and its secret password RAB-BANAIM and its penalties.

I renounce the oaths taken and the curses involved in the Knight of the Ninth Arch of Solomon Degree, and its secret password JEHOVAH used blasphemously and its penalty of having my body given to the beasts of the forest as prey.

I renounce the oaths taken and the curses involved in the Grand Elect, Perfect and Sublime Mason Degree, its secret password, and its penalty of having my body cut open and my bowels given to vultures for food.

I renounce the oaths taken and the curses involved in the Knights of the East Degree, its secret password RAPH-O-DOM, and its penalties.

I renounce the oaths taken and the curses involved in the Prince of Jerusalem Degree, its secret password TEBET-ADAR and its penalty of being stripped naked and having my heart pierced with a poniard.

I renounce the oaths taken and the curses involved in the Knight of the East and West Degree, it secret password ABADDON, and its penalty of incurring the severe wrath of the Almighty Creator of Heaven and Earth.

I renounce the oaths taken and the curses involved in the Council of Kadosh Grand Pontiff Degree, its secret password EMMANUEL used blasphemously and its penalties.

I renounce the oaths taken and the curses involved in the Grand Master of Symbolic Lodges Degree, its secret password JEKSON-STOLKIN, and its penalties.

I renounce the oaths taken and the curses involved in the Noachite of Prussian Knight Degree, its secret password PELEG, and its penalties.

I renounce the oaths taken and the curses involved in the Knight of the Royal Axe Degree, its secret password NOAH-BEZALEEI-SODONIAS, and its penalties.

I renounce the oaths taken and the curses involved in the Chief of the Tabernacle Degree its secret password URIEL-JEHOVAH, and its penalty that I agree the Earth should open up and engulf me up to my neck so I perish.

I renounce the oaths taken and the curses involved in the Prince of the Tabernacle Degree, and its penalty that I should be stoned to death and my body left above ground to rot.

I renounce the oaths taken and the curses involved in the Knight of the Brazen Serpent Degree, its secret password MOSES-JOHANNES, and its penalty that I have my heart eaten by venomous serpents.

I renounce the oaths taken and the curses involved in the Prince of Mercy Degree, its secret passwords, GOMEL, JEHOVAH-JACHIN, and its penalty of condemnation and spite by the entire universe.

I renounce the oaths taken and the curses involved in the Knight Commander of the Temple Degree, its secret password SOLOMON, and its penalty of receiving the severest wrath of Almighty God inflicted upon me.

I renounce the oaths taken and the curses involved in the Knight Commander of the Sun, or Prince Adept Degree, its secret password STIBIUM, and its penalties of having my tongue thrust through with a red-hot iron, of my eyes being plucked out, of my senses of smelling and hearing being removed, of having my hands cut off and in that condition to be left for voracious animals to devour me, or executed by lightning from heaven.

I renounce the oaths taken and the curses involved in the Grand Scottish Knight of Saint Andrew Degree, its secret password NEKAMAH-FURLAC, and its penalties.

30th Degree I renounce the oaths taken and the curses involved in the thirtieth degree of Masonry, the Grand Knight Kadosh and Knight of the Black and White Eagle. I renounce the secret passwords, STIBIUM ALKABAR, PHARASH-KOH and all they mean. In Jesus' name, Amen.

31st Degree I renounce the oaths taken and the curses involved in the thirty-first degree of Masonry, and the Grand Inspector Inquisitor Commander. I renounce all the gods and goddesses of Egypt, which are honored in this degree, including Anubis with the jackals' head, Osiris the Sun god, Isis the sister and wife of Osiris and also the moon goddess. I renounce the Soul of Cheres, the false symbol of immortality, the chamber of the dead and the false teaching of reincarnation and the false god RA. In Jesus' name, Amen.

32nd Degree I renounce the oaths taken and the curses involved in the thirty-second degree of Masonry, and the Sublime Prince of the Royal Secret. I renounce the secret passwords, PHAAL/PARASH-KOL and all they mean. I renounce Masonry's false Trinitarian deity AUM, and its parts, Brahma the creator, Vishnu the preserver and Shiva the destroyer. I renounce the deity of AHURA MAZDA, the claimed spirit and source of all light, and I renounce the worship with fire, which is an abomination to God and also the drinking from a human skull in this and many rites. I also renounce all other Hindu deities and beliefs. In Jesus' name, Amen.

33rd Degree I renounce the oaths taken and the curses involved in the thirty-third degree of Masonry, and the Grand Sovereign Inspector General. I renounce the secret passwords, DEMOLAY, HIRUM ABIFF, FREDERICK OF PRUSSIA, MICHA, MACHA, BEALIM, and ADONAI and all they mean. I renounce all of the former obligations, including having my tongue torn out by its roots, and all other penalties. I renounce and forsake the declaration that Lucifer is God. I renounce the cable-tow around the neck. I renounce the death wish that the wine drunk from a human skull should turn to poison and the skeleton whose cold arms are invited if the oath of this degree is violated. I renounce the three infamous assassins of the grand master, law, property and religion, and I renounce the greed and witchcraft involved in the attempt to manipulate and control the rest of mankind. In Jesus' name, Amen.

Shriners I renounce the oaths taken and the curses involved in the Ancient Arabic Order of the Nobles of the Mystic Shrine. I renounce the piercing of the eyeballs with a three-edged blade, the flaying of the feet, the madness, and the worship of the false god Allah as the god of our fathers. I renounce the hoodwink, the mock hanging, the mock beheading, the mock drinking of the blood of the victim, the mock dog urinating on the initiate, and the offering of urine as a commemoration. In Jesus' name, Amen.

I renounce all the other oaths taken, the rituals of every degree and the curses involved. These include the Allied Degrees, The Red Cross of Constantine, the Order of the Secret Monitor, Knights of Malta, Knights Templar, the Masonic Royal Order of Scotland, Masonic Royal Order of France and Masonic Royal Order of Germany. I renounce all other lodges and secret societies such as Prince Hall Freemasonry. Mormonism, The Order of Amaranth, the Royal Order of Jesters, the Manchester Unity Order of Oddfellows, Buffalos, Druids, Foresters, Orange, Elks, Moose and Eagles Lodges, the Ku Klux Klan, The Grange, the Woodmen of the World. Riders of the Red Robe, the Knights of Pythias, the Mystic Order of the Veiled Prophets of the Enchanted Realm, the women's Orders of the Eastern Star of the Ladies Oriental Shrine, and of the White Shrine of Jerusalem, the girls' order of the Daughters of the Eastern Star, the International Orders of Job's Daughters, and of the Rainbow girls, and the boys' Order of De Molay, and any fraternities or sororities and their effects on me and all my family. In Jesus' name, Amen.

I renounce the ancient pagan teaching and symbolism of the First Tracing Board, the second Tracing board and the Third Tracing Board used in the rituals of the Blue Lodge. I renounce the pagan ritual of the "Point within a Circle" with all its bondages and phallus worship. I renounce the occultic mysticism of the black and white mosaic checkered floor with the tessellated border and five-pointed blazing star or sunburst in the center. I renounce the symbol "G" and it's veiled pagan symbolism and bondages. I renounce and utterly forsake the Great Architect of the Universe, who is revealed in the higher degrees as Lucifer, and his false claim to be the universal fatherhood of God. I also renounce the false claim that Lucifer is the Morning Star and Shining One and I declare that Jesus Christ is the Bright and Morning Star of Revelation 22:16. In Jesus' name, Amen.

I renounce the All-Seeing Third Eye of Freemasonry or Horus in the forehead and its pagan and occult symbolism. I renounce all false communions taken and all mockery of the redemptive work of Jesus Christ on the cross of Calvary, all unbelief, confusion and depression, and all worship of Lucifer as God. I renounce and forsake the lie of Freemasonry that man is not sinful, but merely imperfect, and so can redeem himself through good works. I rejoice that the Bible states that I cannot do a single thing to earn my salvation, but that I can only be saved by grace through faith in Jesus Christ and what He accomplished on the Cross of Calvary. In Jesus' name, Amen.

I renounce all fear of insanity, anguish, death wishes, suicide and death in the name of Jesus Christ. Death was conquered by Jesus Christ, and He alone holds the keys of death and hell. I rejoice that He holds my life in His hands right now. He came to give me life abundantly and eternally, and I believe His promises.

I renounce all anger, hatred, murderous thoughts, revenge, retaliation, spiritual apathy, false religions, and I renounce all unbelief, especially unbelief in the Holy Bible as God's Word, and all compromise of God's Word. I renounce all spiritual searching into false religions, and all striving to please God. I rest in the knowledge that I have found my Lord and Savior Jesus Christ, and that He has found me.

I will burn all objects in my possession which connect me with all lodges and occultic organizations, including Masonry, Witchcraft and Mormonism, including all regalia, aprons, books of rituals, rings and other jewelry. I renounce the effects these or other objects of Masonry, such as the compass, the square, the noose or the blindfold, have had on me or my family. In Jesus' name, Amen.

(1) Symbolically remove the blindfold (hoodwink) and give it to the Lord for disposal; (2) in the same way, symbolically remove the veil of mourning.

(3) Symbolically cut and remove the noose from around the neck, gather it up with the cable -tow running down the body and give it all to the Lord for His disposal.

(4) Symbolically remove the chains and bondages of Freemasonry from your body, (5) Symbolically remove all Freemasonry regalia and armor, especially the Apron; (6) Symbolically remove the ball and chain from the ankles.

I renounce the false Freemasonry marriage covenant, and I now remove from the 4th finger of the right hand the ring of this false marriage covenant, and I give it to the Lord.

I repent of and seek forgiveness for having walked on all unholy ground, including Freemasonry lodges and temples, including any Mormon or other occultic organizations.

I now proclaim that Satan and his demons no longer have any legal rights to mislead and manipulate me. In Jesus' name, Amen.

Holy Spirit, I ask You to show me anything else which I need to do or to pray, so that I and my family may be totally free from the consequences of the sins of Masonry, Witchcraft, Mormonism and Paganism. In Jesus' name, Amen.

Now, Dear Father God, I ask humbly for the blood of Jesus Christ, your Son, to cleanse me from all these sins I have confessed and renounced. To cleanse my spirit, my soul, my mind, will and emotions, and every part of my body which has been affected by these sins. In Jesus' name! Amen.

I renounce every evil spirit associated with Masonry, Witchcraft, Mormonism, and all other sins, and I command in the name of Jesus Christ for Satan and every evil spirit to be bound and to leave me now, touching or harming no-one, never to return to me or my family. I call on the name of the Lord Jesus Christ to be delivered of these spirits in accordance with the many promises of the Bible. I ask to be delivered of every spirit of sickness, and infirmity, and every curse, affliction, addiction, disease, or allergy associated with these sins that I have confessed and renounced. I surrender to God's Holy Spirit and to no other spirit. I ask You Lord, to baptize me in Your Holy Spirit now, according to the promises in Your Word. I take to myself the whole armor of God in accordance with Ephesians Chapter 6, and I rejoice in its protection as Jesus surrounds me and fills me with His Holy Spirit. I enthrone You, Lord Jesus, in my heart, for You are my Lord and my Savior, the source of eternal life. Thank you, Father God, for Your mercy, Your forgiveness, and Your love. In the name of Jesus Christ, Amen.

Modified version of prayer from Unmasking Freemasonry -- Removing the Hoodwink, ISBN 978-1-877463-00-6 by Selwyn R. Stevens (JubileeResources.org)

FULL STOP PRAYER

Father if there is anything between us, knowingly or unknowingly, willingly or unwillingly, forgive me. I clean my heart before You. I plead the blood of Jesus. I open myself to You God, and I ask You, wash me in the blood. Cleanse me by Your grace. Let the blood of Jesus purify me today. God I leave no place for the enemy. This is my season of freedom. This is my season of freedom, Lord! I shall extract, I shall receive what belongs to me by Your word, God. All that you're saying to me - peace, joy, rest, the joy of life! In the kingdom of God on earth - I shall extract that.

I thank You for freeing me right now from every wrong, from every sin, from every iniquity. Oh Lord, I ask You, set me free from that! In Jesus' Name.

Lord Jesus, if I've never said yes to You, let today be that day. I open my heart to You. I believe in You. I ask You to come into my life, make me brand new. Surely You are the Son of God. There is no other. You came and You died. You went to hell for me. And on the third day, You rose again. So that I might live, You died. And today I say to You, "You are my Lord. You are my Savior. You are my Master. You are my King. Have Your way in my life. I thank You for making me brand new!" In Jesus' Mighty Name.

Whatever is not written concerning us must be stopped. In the name of the Lord Jesus! Whatever is not written concerning us must be stopped. Tonight, we put a stop to everything that is not written in Heaven about my life. We make a stop, a stop! We command it to stop! We command it to stop! Whatever is not written concerning my life, according to Heaven, it must stop. Angels of the Lord, we release you right now, to block, to thwart, to destroy, to tear apart, to dismantle, break down, and manifest yourselves into every situation that is not written over my life from Heaven.

For, it is written, my life is written, my life is written, and anything that is not written about my life, in Heaven, while I'm on earth, we command a full stop! We command a full stop. We command a full stop. We release the angels of Heaven, ministering spirits unto the heirs of salvation, flames of fire, sent on our behalf. Oh yes, Lord. Full stop. Full stop, on every situation, on every circumstance that is not written about my life. We command a full stop. We command it to be blocked. We command it to be broken. We command it to be destroyed. We command it to be torn down. Right now, in the name of Jesus Christ. Whenever it came in, whenever it started, whenever it was plotted against me, we release angels of the Lord to go into that day, to go into that moment, and tear it apart. Tear it up, break it down. Every plan of the wicked one over my life, it shall not happen, it will not be. We stop it tonight, we break it tonight, we cut it off tonight, we render it powerless tonight.

Every wicked word, every lie of the enemy, every plot, every plan of the enemy of my destiny, we cut it off, we block it, we break it, we shut it down, in the mighty name of Jesus.

Lord, if it is not written about my life, I shall not have it, I shall not have it, I shall not have it, I shall not have it. Oh Lord, if it is not written in the realm of Heaven over my life, it shall not be for me. It shall not be for me. We break it up, we shut it down, in the mighty name of Jesus. We send the Word into our life, into our generation, and every plot, every plan of the wicked one to maim, to destroy, to cut us short, we block it, we stop it, we break it. We break it! Tonight, in the mighty name of the Lord Jesus Christ. Everything that affects our destiny, everything that affects our purpose, we block it, we stop it, in the name of Jesus Christ.

We send out Heaven's warriors on our behalf right now. We release you, we release you, we release you, into the time of our life, into the time of our parents' life, into the time of our grandparents' life, we release you wherever the plot, wherever the plan, wherever the enemy ever started working against my destiny. We cut it out, we box it up, we throw it away. It shall not happen; the devil's plan is a busted plan. It will not work in my life. In the mighty name of the Lord Jesus Christ.

GENERATIONAL CURSES PRAYER

1. I confess the sins of my ancestors, my parents, and my own sin of _____. (category)

2. I choose to forgive and release them; for the sin, the curses, and the consequences in my life.

3. I ask you to forgive me Lord, for this sin; for yielding to it and to the resulting curses. I receive your forgiveness.

4. On the basis of your forgiveness Lord, I choose to forgive myself for involvement in this sin.

5. I renounce the sin and curses of _____. (list)

6. I break this power from my life and the lives of my descendants through the redemptive work of Christ on the cross.

7. I receive God's freedom from this sin and from the resulting curses. I receive _____. (an opposite)

Make a list of opposites and make them part of your daily devotions for at least 40 days. Receive them daily.

Acknowledgement for this prayer is given to Chester and Betsy Kylstra, Proclaiming His Word Publishing, restoringthefoundations.org Used by permission

GENERATIONAL CURSES

Abandonment & Rejection

Abdication

Blocked Intimacy

Desertion

Divorce

Isolation

Loneliness

Neglect

Separation

Self-pity

Victimization

Expected Rejection

Perceived Rejection

Self-Rejection

Rejection of God

Rejection of others

Poor Stewardship

Bankruptcy

Cheating

Covetousness

Debt

Deception

Delinquency

Dishonesty

Failure

Greed

Idolatry of Possessions

Irresponsible Spending

Irresponsibility

Job Failures

Job Losses

- continue to next column

Poor Stewardship

Lack

Laziness

Neglect

Poverty

Procrastination

Robbery

Robbing God

Stealing

Stinginess

Drug dealing

Gambling

Organized Crime

Anxiety & Fears

Burden

False Responsibility

Fatigue

Heaviness

Nervousness

Restlessness

Weariness

Bewilderment

Dread

Harassment

Horror Movies

Intimidation

Mental Torment

Over-Sensitivity

Paranoia

Phobia

Superstition

- continue to next column

Anxiety & Fears

Worry

Fear of Authorities

Fear of being Abused

Fear of being Attacked

Fear of being Wrong

Fear of being a Victim

Fear of Cancer

Fear of Death

Fear of Diabetes

Fear of Demons

Fear of Exposure

Fear of Failure

Fear of Heart Attack

Fear of Inadequacy

Fear of Infirmities

Fear of Loss

Fear of Man

Fear of Performing

Fear of Poverty

Fear of Public Speaking/ Singing

Fear of Reading out loud

Fear of Punishment

Fear of Rejection

Fear of Sexual Inadequacy

Fear of Sexual Perversion

Fear of Success

Fear of Violence

Fear of Not Being Good Enough

Fear of Not Having Fear

Unhealthy Fear of God

Anger, Rage & Violence

Abandonment

Feuding

Frustration

Hatred

Hostility

Murder

Punishment

Rage

Resentment

Retaliation

Revenge

Spoiled Little Boy/Girl

Temper Tantrums

Violence

Abuse

Arguing

Bickering

Cruelty

Cursing

Death

Destruction

Hate

- continue to next column

Mocking

Murder/Abortion

Retaliation

Strife

Torture/Mutilation

Deception & Rebellion

Blindness

Cheating/Stealing

Confusion

Denial

Fraudulence

Infidelity

Lying

Secretiveness

Self-Deception

Treachery

Treason

Trickery

Untrustworthiness

Contempt

Deception

Defiance

Independence

- continue to next column

Disobedience

Independence

Insubordination

Resistance

Self-Sufficiency

Self-Will

Stubbornness

Undermining

A Religious spirit

Antichrist

Betrayal

Denominationalism

Division

Hypocrisy

Injustice

Legalism

Liberalism

New Age practices

Religiosity

Excessive rules

Spiritual pride

Traditionalism

Formalism

Ritualism

Unworthiness & Unbelief

Inadequacy
Inferiority
Insecurity
Self-Accusation
Self-Condemnation
Self-Hate
Self-Punishment
Apprehension
Double-Mindedness
Doubt
Fear of being Wrong
Mind Blocking
Mistrust
Rationalism
Skepticism
- continue to next column

Bitterness

Accusation
Blaming
Complaining
Condemnation
Criticalness
Gossip
Judging
Murmuring
Ridicule
Slander
Unforgiveness

Suspicion
Uncertainty

Manipulation & Control

Appeasement
Denial
Domineering
Double Binding
Enabling
False Responsibility
Female Control
Occult Control/Jezebel
Passive Aggression
Passivity/Ahab
Possessiveness
Always right
Stubbornness
Witchcraft

Pride & Mocking

Arrogance
Conceit
Controlling
Egotistical
Haughtiness
Leviathan
Prejudice
Self-Centeredness
Self-Importance
Vanity
Blaspheming
Cursing
Laughing
Profanity
Ridicule
Sarcasm
Scorn

Shame

Abandonment
Anger
Bad Boy/Girl
Condemnation
Defilement
Different
Disgrace
Embarrassment
Guilt
Hatred
Inferiority
Illegitimacy
Occult Involvement
Self-Accusation
Self-Hate
Self-Pity

Performance & Failure

Extreme Competition
Driving Zeal
Envy
Jealousy
People Pleasing
Perfectionism
Possessiveness
Rivalry
Striving
Workaholism
Boom/Bust Cycle
Defeat
Loss
Performance
Pressure to Succeed

Infirmities/Disease

Accidents (falls, cars, etc)
Anorexia/Bulimia/Gluttony
Arthritis
Asthma —allergies & hay fever
Barrenness/Miscarriage
Bone/Joint Problems
Cancer
Congestion/in lungs
Diabetes
Fatigue
Female Problems
Mental Illness
MS
Migraines/Mind Binding
Physical Abnormalities
Premature Death
Graves Disease
T.B. & emphysema
Autism
Hypochondria
A bent body and spine
Chemical imbalance
High Fever
Bi-polar
Impotent – frail & lame
Arthritis & a root of bitterness
All oppression
Pain and affliction
All lingering disorders
Tumors & cysts
Weakness – tiredness &
   Fatigue
- continue to next column

All infections (viral &
   bacterial)
Epilepsy & seizures
Fear of infirmity &
disease

Addictions, Escape & Dependencies

Cocaine
Downers/Uppers
Marijuana
Non-Prescription Drugs
Prescription Drugs
Street Drugs
Tranquilizers
Alcohol
Caffeine
Cigarettes
Computers
Food
Gambling
Internet
Pornography
Overspending
Sex
Sports
Television
Video Games
Movies
Music
Daydreaming
Fantasy
Forgetfulness
Hopelessness
Isolation
- continue to next column

Laziness
Passivity
Procrastination
Sleep/Slumber/
Oversleeping
Trance
Withdrawal

Mental Problems & Depression

Craziness
Compulsions
Confusion
Distraction
Forgetfulness
Hallucinations
Hysteria
Insanity
Mind Binding
Mind Blocking
Paranoia
Mind Racing
Schizophrenia
Senility
Dejection
Discouragement
Despair
Despondency
Gloominess
Hopelessness
Insomnia
Misery
Oversleeping
Sadness
Self-Pity
Suicide Fantasies
Withdrawal

Sexual Sins & Perversion

Abortion
Adultery
Bestiality
Demonic Sex
Defilement/Uncleanness
Exposure
Fantasy Lust
Fornication
Flirtation
Frigidity
Homosexuality
Illegitimacy
Incest
Incubus
Lesbianism
Lewdness
Lust/Fantasy Lust
Pre-Marital Sex
Masturbation
molestation
Pornography
Prostitution/Harlotry
Rape
Seduction/Alluring/
    Enticing
Sexual Abuse
Sodomy
S & M
Succubus
All ungodly soul ties

Witchcraft & the Occult

Abortion
Molech & Baal
Ahab
Animal Spirits
- continue to next column

Antichrist
Astral Projection
Astrology
Automatic Writing
Behemoth
Black Magic
Occult/Witchcraft Books
Crystal Ball
Death, Suicide
Conjuring Demons
Dispatching Demons
Demon Worship
Divination
Eight Ball
Evil Eye
ESP
False Gifts (Occult)
Fascination with evil
Fortune Telling
Handwriting Analysis
Hexing
Horoscopes
Hypnosis
I Ching
All Idolatry
Incantations
Jezebel
Levitation
Leviathan
Mediumship
Mental Telepathy
Necromancy
Non-Christian Exorcism
Ouija Board
Palm Reading
Past Life Readings
Pendulum Readings
Psychic Readings
Psychic Healing
- continue to next column

Python
Reincarnation
Satanic Worship
Seances
Slavery, Occult
Sorcery
Spells
Spirit Guides
Spiritism
Superstition
Table Tipping
Tarot Cards
Tea Leaf Reading
Third Eye, Using
Trance
TM
Vampire
Occult Victim
Voodoo
Water Witching
Werewolf
White Magic
Wicca
Meditation, Eastern
Evil music
Evil videos & movies
Evil games
Dungeon & Dragons
Martial Arts
Yoga

Victim, Trauma & Grief

Appeasement
Betrayal
Deportation
Entrapped
Helplessness
Hopelessness
- continue to next column

Victim, Trauma & Grief

Mistrust

Passivity

Self-pity

Suspicion

Trauma

Unfaithfulness

All Forms of Abuse, incl.

Emotional, Physical

Mental, Sexual

Spiritual & Verbal

Accident

Loss

Imprisoned

Rape

Torture

Violence

Agony

Anguish

Crying

Despair

GIFTING PRAYER

Heavenly Father, I desire to come into the fullness of the identity you have given me. I realize that things I have said and done, and things that have been said and done to me, have affected my freedom to express what You want to say and do through me. You are a creative God, and I want to look and sound like You, Heavenly Father.

I renounce and repent for agreeing with the enemy and believing his lies that I don't have good ideas, that my voice is not needed, or that I'm stuck. I renounce and break the power of perfectionism. I renounce any need to prove myself. I renounce the belief that God short-changed me when He made me. I renounce any belief that He is harsh or has unfair expectations of me. I break the power of every word curse, spoken or unspoken, by me or anyone else, over my life.

Lord, I ask that You reveal any vows or judgments I have made that keep me from being comfortable with my identity, flowing in my gifts, or being creative. (Listen for and break agreement with these.) I renounce, repent, and break all agreement with the spirit of death - death to my ministry, dreams, or anointing.

I choose to believe that I have something important to contribute in the Kingdom of God, that my voice is needed. God has placed a unique expression of His nature in my very DNA, and He desires for me to become everything He made me to be. I give myself permission to be different from anyone else, to stand out. I will no longer listen to lies that steal away my worth and identity. I agree with the truth that I am valuable because Jesus died and rose from the dead for me. I am a son/daughter of God, and I belong to Him. I choose to believe that I was created in God's image and therefore am a creative person. I believe and receive the gifts given to me by Holy Spirit, and I earnestly desire His gifts in greater measure in my life. I give myself permission to dream, and to allow God to do big things in and through me. I am made in the image of God and commanded to take dominion over the earth. I listen for the way God wants things to be and I am obedient to His voice. The power of God flows through my life to make Earth become like Heaven, just like Jesus prayed for.

Holy Spirit, I receive everything you want to give me. I ask You for creative ideas, business ideas, ideas for my family, train me in the skills that I need to do what You called me to do. I ask you for godly mentors, who will be able to impart to me the gifts, character, and anointing that you desire for me to walk in. I receive the ability to learn things supernaturally.

Just as you blessed Shadrach, Meshach and Abednego and it was said they were 10 times better than any of their peers because of the Lord's voice in their life, I receive that excellence, favor, and the power of the Holy Spirit to do what God has assigned me to do. I receive the baptism of the Holy Spirit and fire that John the Baptist promised Jesus would bring, so that everything and everyone my life touches will be touched by the power of God.

Lord, I want to discover everything You created me to be, guided by Holy Spirit, for Your glory. I yield myself to You, Lord. Show me how to let Your Spirit flow through me, to bring Heaven to Earth. In Jesus' mighty name, Amen.

HEARING GOD'S VOICE PRAYER

We use this prayer for people who have trouble hearing God's voice. The blockage can be related to false teaching, anger towards God, things people said…let the Holy Spirit break the strongholds and take them to the memories that caused them to stop hearing Him.

This prayer is powerful because of your faith. Pray with sincerity and power, make the prayer your own. Let the Holy Spirit show you anyone you need to forgive, who has contributed to blockages in hearing God's Voice.

Father, I renounce and repent for any wrong beliefs or unbeliefs I've had about hearing Your voice. I believe that You can speak to us in many ways: through Scripture, through Your voice, through sensing in my spirit, through signs and wonders, and through visions. I am a child of God. You love me unconditionally, which means no matter what I do or don't do, You love me. You desire to fellowship with me. I am chosen by You and I have a purpose. I am worthy, and I am a carrier of Your powerful Holy Spirit. I give the Holy Spirit permission to minister to me, to heal and break everything that gets in the way of hearing God's voice.

I renounce and repent for any and all fear that is blocking Your voice. I will not fear hearing some other voice and confusing it for Your voice. I trust myself, as a powerful child of God, that I hear Your voice. I trust You, and what You say. I trust Your promise that when I ask for something good, I will not get something evil instead, because I am Your son/daughter. I command my emotions and all my senses to come underneath the power of the Holy Spirit. I renounce all fear of not hearing Your voice. I break all noise that blocks me from hearing. I break any confusion that comes when I try to listen. I come out of agreement with any spirit of religion or false teaching that says You do not speak today. I renounce and break all insecurity, fear, and ungodly beliefs that hold me back from hearing You the way I was created to hear You. Holy Spirit, I give You permission to heal all trauma and wounds in my life, so that I can walk in my identity of being Your son/daughter.

I renounce any unhealthy fear of God and the spirit realm. I declare Your Word over my life that says You have plans to prosper me and not to harm me, to give me hope and a future. I receive it in Jesus' powerful name.

Father, through Your Holy Spirit, I invite you to speak to me. I want to know You, and have You know me. I want to follow Your voice. Teach me to recognize the Holy Spirit, and the ways You speak to me. I give permission to the power of the Holy Spirit to teach me my discernment, what is flesh, and what is spirit. "For our struggle is not against flesh and blood, but against the rulers, against the authorities, against the powers of this dark world and against the spiritual forces of evil in the heavenly realms" Eph 6:12. I choose to believe and declare that hearing Your voice is my portion and my destiny. From this day forward, You will teach me and train me, and I will be built up in You. You are my strong tower and my fortress. In the powerful name of Jesus, Amen.

If you feel like there is wounding or past trauma that has kept you from hearing God's voice, we suggest you go through inner healing. The Lord can heal that place of trauma and you can begin to hear His voice.

Inner Healing: Holy Spirit, please take me to the place where I stopped hearing God's voice…

See Steps for Inner Healing for help in ministering.

ISLAM PRAYER

Lord God, I confess that I have sinned and turned away from you. I repent and turn towards Christ as my Savior and Lord. Please forgive me specifically for any times when I have intimidated others, or sought to impose inferiority or humiliation on others. Forgive me for all my pride. Forgive me for any times when I have abused or dominated others. I renounce all these things in Jesus' name.

Lord, I praise you for the gift of forgiveness by Christ on the cross. I acknowledge that you have accepted me. I thank you that through the cross I am reconciled to you and to others. I declare today that I am your child and an inheritor of the Kingdom of God.

Father, I agree with you that I am not subject to fear, but I am a child of your love. I reject and renounce the demands of Islam as taught by Muhammad. I renounce all forms of submission to 'Allah of the Quran', and declare that I worship the God and Father of our Lord Jesus Christ and Him alone.

I repent for the sins of my ancestors for submitting to the dhimma pact and its principles, and I ask your forgiveness for their sins.

I renounce and revoke all pacts of surrender made by myself, or my ancestors to the community and principles of Islam.

I completely reject the dhimma and every one of its conditions. I renounce the blow on the neck in the jizya payment ritual, together with all that it represents. I specifically renounce the curse of decapitation and curse of death symbolized by this ritual.

I declare that the dhimma pact is nailed to the cross of Christ. The dhimma has been made a public spectacle, and has no power or rights over me. I declare that the spiritual principles of the dhimma pact are exposed, disarmed, defeated and disgraced through the cross of Christ.

I renounce false feelings of gratitude to Islam.

I renounce false feelings of guilt or compassion.

I renounce deception and lies.

I renounce all agreements to keep silent about my faith in Christ.

I renounce all agreements to keep silent about the dhimma or Islam.

I will speak and I will not be silent.

I declare that according to John 8:32 "the truth shall set me free" and I choose to live as a free person in Christ Jesus.

I renounce and cancel all curses spoken against me and my family in the name of Islam.

I renounce and cancel all curses spoken against my ancestors.

I specifically renounce and break the curse of death. Death, you have no power over me!

I declare that these curses have no power over me.

I claim the blessings of Christ as my spiritual inheritance.

I renounce intimidation. I choose to be bold in Christ Jesus.

I renounce manipulation and control.

I renounce abuse and violence.

I renounce slavery.

I specifically renounce all oppression of women and children.

I renounce all fear.

I renounce the fear of being rejected.

I renounce the fear of losing my property and possessions.

I renounce the fear of poverty.

I renounce the fear of being enslaved.

I renounce the fear of rape.

I renounce the fear of being isolated.

I renounce the fear of losing my family.

I renounce the fear of being killed and the fear of death.

I renounce the fear of Islam. I renounce the fear of Muslims.

I renounce the fear of being involved in public or political activity.

I declare that Jesus Christ is Lord of all.

I submit to Jesus as the Lord of every area of my life.

Jesus Christ is Lord of my home. Jesus Christ is Lord of my city. Jesus Christ is Lord of my nation.

Jesus Christ is Lord of all peoples in this land. I submit to Jesus Christ as my Lord.

I renounce humiliation. I declare that Christ has accepted me. I serve Him and Him alone.

I renounce all shame. I declare that through the cross I am cleansed from all sin. Shame has no rights over me and I will reign with Christ in glory.

Lord, forgive me and my ancestors for all hatred toward Muslims. I renounce hatred towards Muslims and all other people, and declare the love of Christ for Muslims and all other people on this earth.

I repent of the sins of the church and of wrongful submission of church leaders.

I renounce alienation. I declare that I am forgiven and accepted by God through Christ. I am reconciled to God. No power in heaven or on earth can make any charge against me before the throne of God.

I declare my praise and thanks to God our Father, to Christ who is my only Savior, and to the Holy Spirit who alone gives me life.

I commit myself to be a living witness to Jesus Christ as Lord and Savior. I am not ashamed of His cross. I am not ashamed of His resurrection.

I declare I am a child of the living God, the God of Abraham, Isaac and Jacob.

I declare the victory of God and of His Messiah. I declare that every knee will bow and every tongue will confess that Jesus Christ is Lord.

I declare forgiveness towards Muslims for practicing the system of dhimmitude.

Father God, please free me from the dhimma, the spirit of dhimmitude, and every ungodly principle attached to the dhimma pact.

I ask now that you fill me with your Holy Spirit, and pour upon me all the blessings of the Kingdom of Jesus Christ. Grant me grace to understand the truth of your Word clearly and to apply it in every area of my life.

Grant to me words of hope and life, and bless my lips so I can speak them to others with authority and power in Jesus' name.

Give me the boldness to be a faithful witness of Christ. Grant me a deep love for Muslim people and a passion to share the love of Christ with them.

I declare and ask these things in the name of Jesus Christ my Lord and Savior.

Amen.

Modified version of prayer from Discerning the Past to See the End Times, ISBN 978-1-877463-91-4 by Selwyn R. Stevens (JubileeResources.org)

PRAYER TO BREAK POVERTY

Father God, I come to you in the name of Your son Jesus Christ, and I repent for the sins of my ancestors all the way back through my bloodlines, to the third and fourth generations, even back to Adam and Eve. I repent for my disobedience to Your voice in my life. I repent for pushing You away, trusting in myself, and relying on my ways to establish my life. I repent for any way I listened to the enemy, instead of listening to You and Your Word. I repent for any way I have desired my flesh and the things of the flesh, instead of You and the Holy Spirit. Father God, I receive forgiveness for these sins, and redemption from all curses associated with these sins. I receive and apply the blood of Jesus Christ the Messiah, to break all generational rebellion and poverty on my bloodlines and off of my life, in Jesus Name.

Father God, I repent for any of my ancestors who offered sacrifices to any false god. I repent for any withholding of the tithe, the first fruits and the best portions, and for all fear, wrong motives, and attitudes, of their hearts and mine. Lord God, please bring peace and submission to God into my bloodline right now.

Father God, I break any curses of Cain against my bloodline. I renounce and break all jealousy against my brother, all coveting and envy. I repent for rebellion, anger, and murder in my generational bloodline. God, please restore the authority over land, and the promise of land, and restore Your promises and fruitfulness on my life. Lord, remove any mark put on my bloodline, and break all curses of wandering.

I repent for my ancestors and for myself, for any way I denied justice to the poor, for oppressing widows and the fatherless, for holding resentment, or any unforgiveness to another brother or sister. I break all curses spoken against me and my finances or destiny, by others or myself. Hear my prayers, open my heart and ear gates and eye gates again, in the powerful name of Jesus Christ.

I repent for generational dishonesty and taking advantage, selfishness, pride, stinginess, bad business deals, and all justification of dishonesty to bless my own life.

I ask for forgiveness and choose to forgive my ancestors who refuse to forgive debt. I repent for a hard heart and a tight fist. Lord, I repent for all ancestors who were unfaithful, greedy, and disobedient. I repent for ancestors who were thieves and liars. I repent for breaking covenant, and for coveting. Lord God, restore mercy, and give me a heart of cheerful giving. I receive Your blessings and favor into my family line. I receive the blessing of being Your chosen people, and I desire to be in covenant with You.

Father God, I repent for not serving You with a joyful heart, for complaining, and not trusting You. Forgive me for fearing money more than fearing and respecting You and Your commands. I renounce fear of money, fear of lack, and fear of neglect, in Jesus Name. I declare You fill my barns and they overflow.

Lord, please break all curses of destruction against us from the locusts, worms, fire, loss, or sinking. Please break a slavery mindset, set all sons and daughters free, and stop all destruction and chaos. Lord, please remove iron yokes, all blindness, oppression, and robbing spirits. I renounce and break all curses of hunger, nakedness, poverty, and slavery.

Lord, I also repent for any of my ancestors who put up security or pledges for another. Please forgive me or my ancestors for unfulfilled debts. I break all ungodly covenants, oaths, and alliances. Lord, please remove all traps or snares from my words or others. Please break all sluggard and slumbering spirits from me and restore wisdom and Godly ambition. I renounce and break all generational laziness, neglect, and lack of Godly judgement. I repent for spiritual pride and family members who refuse to repent. I repent for myself and my generations for chasing fantasies. I renounce and break all curses of poverty. I break and renounce illegitimacy in me or my family.

I repent for all ignoring of discipline and correction. I repent for all greed, all bribes, and for all idle talk and all boasting. I repent for not keeping Your Word. Lord I renounce and break shunning and all division. I break walls between me and others. Please restore honor to my family, Lord. I repent for all rejection of God, and any cursing or blasphemy of God. I renounce all poverty thinking, and poverty acts that block blessings.

Lord, I repent for me and my ancestors who followed deceptive words and relied on their social or religious identity for salvation. I repent for idolatry, ungodly sacrifices or worship, as well as innocent bloodshed, disobedience, and pride. I repent for trying to please man instead of God. I repent for accepting praise, worship, ungodly authority, and titles from men. I renounce religious spirits of legalism, self exaltation, and hypocrisy. Lord, restore wholeness, wholeheartedness, and a pure heart, and make me noble, faithful, and sensitive to You.

I renounce and break all generational alliances with the Babylonian System. I renounce and break all ties to this worldly system, and all its benefits. Lord, I break all connections and control that the queen of Heaven (the false goddess Ashtoreth) has on my family line and me. Lord I break all ungodly oaths, covenants, pledges, and dedications. I apply the blood of Jesus to all the roots of iniquity. I repent for ancestors who did not believe or declare Jesus is Lord.

Father God, remove any curse that keeps me from enjoying the fruits of my labor. I renounce and break all curses that say there will never be enough. Lord, restore a new purse, one without holes. I receive and choose to believe I have the mind of Christ in the matters of finance. I declare I am grafted in with the blood of Jesus Christ, into a new family line and I choose to live by the Kingdom of God.

Holy Spirit, I give You permission to rewire me inside and out, to live by God's systems and using the Word of God as my life's guidance, putting it first. I receive my inheritance as a child of God. I will live as His child. I now renounce and break a spirit of poverty and lack, as well as all slavery mentalities and spirits, they must go now.

I receive the Holy Spirit's guidance and the spirit of wisdom as God grows me and prospers me in Jesus' name, Amen

REJECTION PRAYER

Heavenly Father, I desire that the stronghold of rejection be broken from my life. In the name of Jesus, I repent of every sin, known and unknown, that has given the spirit of rejection power in my life. I also break every generational curse of rejection, and I repent for the sins of my forefathers and foremothers back to the third, fourth, even the tenth generation and beyond. I speak to rejection, and I break your power over my life, in Jesus' powerful name.

Heavenly Father, I repent for all fear that I have allowed to dominate my life, and I renounce the fear of being rejected by You, and being rejected by others. I break all fear of rejection in my life.

Heavenly Father, I choose to love myself and to see myself as You see me - a beautiful and holy bride. I repent of trying to be like others and quenching my own personality. I repent for agreeing with the spirit of self-rejection that says You don't love me and that I shouldn't love myself. In Jesus name, I renounce you, spirit of self-rejection, and I break your power over my life. I plead the precious blood of Jesus over my life right now.

Rejection of others, I have repented and I have forgiven, and I now renounce you, and I break your hold on my life, in Jesus' name.

Heavenly Father, I repent of all rejection of You, and all rejection of the gift of Your Son, the Lord Jesus Christ. I have looked at things around me to show me if You love me or not, and that was wrong. From this day forward, I will look only to Jesus, and His sacrificial death, as evidence and proof of Your Love and acceptance of me. Spirit of rejection, you will no longer manipulate or control my life, in Jesus' holy name. I am not rejected! I am loved and accepted! It is finished! In Jesus' powerful name. Amen.

SEXUAL IMPRINTING PRAYER

God wants to restore your sexuality. There is hope in Jesus Christ, and He wants to heal every part of your identity.

There is a core of sexual imprinting with each person's trauma. They have been imprinted wrongly and God wants to minister to that imprinting and bring healing, release, purity, and hope. We want to give people God's complete healing, not another coping mechanism.

Client needs to have worked through any unforgiveness, see Forgiveness homework for help.

Prayer:

Lord, we pray for cleansing and restoration. We break the power of every kind of trauma and abuse that has caused_____(person's name)_____ to hold on to ungodly ways for comfort. We break the legal right and the trauma that perverted _____'s sexual imprint, and we renounce and break every addiction that came in through this trauma or abuse. Lord, we break every ungodly soul tie that is connected to _____'s sexual experience. We pray for restoration of spiritual virginity and purity. We pray, Lord, that you would come and wipe his/her sexual slate clean, restore to_____'s body and to his/her memory wholesome pictures and imprints so that he/she will be completely free in mind, body, and spirit.

We loose_____'s sexuality to the Lord to be completely healed and sealed. In Jesus' powerful name, Amen.

1 Thessalonians 5:23, "May God Himself, the God who makes everything holy and whole, make you holy and whole, put you together, spirit, soul, and body, and keep you fit for the coming of our Master, Jesus Christ."

Healing: Ask the person to close their eyes and picture themselves, then ask Jesus how He sees them.

Dealing with sexual strongholds:

We want to pray over the person, breaking all strongholds that are related to sexual imprinting. Example: We pull down the strongholds of lust (of the eyes and flesh), fantasy, pornography, masturbation, homosexuality, unclean spirits, seduction, rejection, self-hate, all things that come from abuse, etc., and cast them out.

SHAME PRAYER

Heavenly Father, I repent for agreeing with the enemy and believing his lies, that I am an evil person, that I am bad, that I am different from others, that I don't fit in, or that I am dirty, and that I am not worthy. I repent of trying to hide myself from You, and from others. I repent of not believing that the blood of Jesus can cleanse me from all the sin and shame of my past, and from all the things I have done, and all the things that have been done to me. I repent for not believing Your Word and not accepting Your cleansing, and your love. I renounce all shame as a work of the devil designed to rob me of joy, and of an open relationship with You Lord, and with other people.

I renounce shame as a tactic and a tool of the enemy to keep me from being the person You created me to be. I choose to be free of all shame, to receive my full release from all the shame of my past. I break all agreements I have made with the lying voice of shame. I break all soul ties and every generational tie that would bind me in any way to shame. I break all curses, spoken or unspoken, over my life, by myself or others. I break every vow and covenant, every contract and every agreement that would give shame any power in my life.

Lord, I come to You now for Your healing touch. Thank You for releasing me from all the shame of my past, everything that I've done and everything that has happened to me. In Jesus' powerful name, Amen.

I declare over myself Proverbs 31:25, "Strength and honor are her clothing she shall rejoice in time to come." Genesis 1:27, "God created man in His own image, in the image of God He created him, male and female He created them." In Jesus' name.

SONSHIP PRAYER

Parents

Heavenly Father, I bring my parents to you, in the name of Jesus Christ. I want to be free. I don't want to walk in rebellion. I don't want to fear Godly submission anymore in my life. I want to walk in the freedom of Sonship. I bring my relationship with my father and mother to You. I choose to forgive them for every way they misrepresented Your heart and love for me, the heart of a true Father. I forgive them for their inability to be affectionate. I forgive them for not being gentle with me, or neglecting me. I forgive them for not being trustworthy. I choose to release them.

Dad/Mom, I ask you to forgive me for any way I rebelled against being parented. I looked at your faults and saw weakness and pain in your lives and I judged you because of it. I dishonored you in my heart and closed my heart to you. I stopped receiving from you. I justified my choices because of the weaknesses I saw in your lives. I don't want to do that anymore. I renounce all rebellion against love. I renounce all rebellion against being parented. I renounce fear that closed my spirit.

I choose to open my spirit, to no longer be controlled by fear. I release you, Dad/Mom, from the need I've had that you make things right with me. This isn't about you setting it right, or about your faults. This is about me and the spirit of sonship. I bring you to the foot of the cross and place the cross between you and me. Lord, I ask that the cross filter out every hurt and disappointment, so only honor and love remain.

Father, please forgive me for every sin of dishonor I committed towards my parents. I renounce all dishonor towards them. I renounce any curse that came upon my life through dishonor. (Mal. 4:6) In Jesus' powerful name.

Spouse/Romantic Relationship or Parent _____ (insert any relationship that applies)

Lord, I bring to You my husband or wife, or any past relationship with a man or woman. I choose to forgive them for the ways they misrepresented God's love. I forgive them for any way they devalued me, and brought confusion in my identity. I forgive all abuse - sexual, verbal, emotional, physical, and spiritual. I forgive them for controlling or manipulating me. I forgive them for putting me down, for making me feel unworthy or unwanted. I forgive them for any way they treated me like I wasn't enough, or I was too much.

Thank You Lord, for the truth that you are not a man that You would lie. I renounce the ways I have associated men's or a father's behavior with God's behavior. I choose to surrender any walls that I built to protect myself, and I choose to forgive. These walls keep me from Your love, Lord. I don't want them there anymore.

I trust You to teach me Godly boundaries and behavior in my relationships. I ask that You heal and restore my attitude toward men or fathers, so I can walk in healthy intimacy.

In the powerful name of Jesus.

Employers

Father, I bring past and present employers to You. The hurt and confusion from my parents has carried over into my workplace, but I don't want it there anymore. I want a spirit of honor. I want a spirit of Godly submission - one that is based on my heart attitude and not others' behavior.

I choose to forgive any employers who haven't been sensitive to my needs. I forgive them for passing me over, for promoting others. I forgive them for being harsh with me. I forgive them for putting me down. I choose to forgive them for misrepresenting God's love.

I renounce all rebellion I had towards employers. I renounce all poverty that came into my life. Lord, You created me to receive favor and inheritance. I renounce all rebellion in my workplace. I renounce manipulation and control to get my boss to promote or honor me. I renounce seeking the praise of men. I choose to believe that God is my source, and He provides for me financially, because He loves me unconditionally, and cares for me daily. I declare that as I go to work, I'll have a new spirit - the spirit of Christ flowing through me, in Jesus' name.

Spiritual Authorities

Lord, I bring to You the spiritual leaders in my life from the past and the present. Forgive me for the ways my unhealed father/mother issues affected these relationships in my life. I had ungodly beliefs towards my parents, and they carried over towards spiritual leaders in my life. I don't want to do that anymore. I want this broken off my life.

I choose to forgive them for every way they misrepresented God's love. I forgive them for their inability to nurture or mentor me. I forgive them for not being sensitive to my needs. I renounce all manipulation, to get leaders to promote or honor me. I renounce seeking the praise of man. I renounce rebellion against authority, and I choose to forgive them. I lay them at the foot of the cross. Let the cross filter out all hurt and all pain, so that only honor and love remains.

Father God, release the spirit of sonship in me, a spirit of honor, a spirit of Godly submission. I choose to honor the spiritual authorities You have set in place in my life. Thank You for the ways that You bless my life through their involvement. I choose to open my heart and spirit to receive all inheritance You have for my life. Show me ways to honor, promote, and bless the leaders in my life. I accept the spirit of sonship right now, in Jesus' name.

God

Father, forgive me for lacking a spirit of sonship towards You. I have wanted things my way, and I didn't like it when You wouldn't let me have my way. Forgive me for blaming others, blaming You, and rebelling against You. Forgive me for trying to protect myself, and believing that You were not with me. Forgive me for believing I had to earn Your love. I renounce the orphan spirit. I renounce the slave mentality. I receive You as my Father; I choose to be Your child. Thank You for loving me so much.

Directions to start Inner Healing, if needed, see Steps for Inner Healing:

Holy Spirit, at what moment did I cease being a son or daughter? Please take me to that memory, to heal it.

SOUL TIES PRAYER

Heavenly Father, I submit myself completely to You. I ask You to forgive me for all sexual misconduct or ungodly relationships with _____ (everyone on this list). And in the powerful name of Jesus, I ask that my spirit be loosed from them, according to Matthew 18:18-19, and I tell my spirit to forget the unions. I tell my mind to release responsibility for them, and I tell my emotions to let go and forget all attachment. I tell the fragmented pieces of my soul to come back together and be whole. I choose to forgive every person that I have been involved with in any wrong way. I break every ungodly soul tie in Jesus' name.

Lord, I renounce all use of my body as an instrument of unrighteousness. I ask You to break all bondages that Satan has brought into my life through these ungodly soul ties. I repent and confess my participation, and I choose to forgive myself. I choose to no longer be angry with myself or punish myself for these sins. I receive Your forgiveness and Your cleansing. I now present my body to You as a living sacrifice, holy and acceptable to You. I reserve the sexual use of my body only for marriage. I renounce the lie of Satan that my body is not clean, that it is dirty, or in any way unacceptable as a result of my past sexual experience.

Lord, I thank You that you have cleansed and forgiven me, that You love and accept me unconditionally. I choose to accept myself, and my body as cleansed. In Jesus' powerful name, Amen.

Acknowledgment is given to Teresa Castleman's book "Brownsville Deliverance Manual" 1996-97

TRAUMA PRAYER

Lord Jesus, Prince of Peace, please come and bring peace to me/name right now.

You have not given me/name a spirit of fear, but of love, power, and a sound mind, and I claim that for him/her/myself today. I ask that the power of the Holy Spirit would go layer by layer, through my/name's soul, drawing out all trauma, fear, shock, pain, and shame. Jesus, you suffered and died for me/name, and I/we claim and receive all that you accomplished for him/her/me. Remove the trauma from any memories stored in the cells of my/name's body, and restore his/her/my cells to perfect order and vibration.

Lord, I bless my/name's conception, I bless every moment I/name was in his/her/my mother's womb, and I bless his/her/my birth. I ask Lord, that You would restore the original DNA. Please restore all vibrations and frequencies to their original God-created design, and remove anything that is not of You. I/We place the cross of Jesus Christ between my/name and my/his/her generational line, and ask that all iniquity be forgiven and canceled from his/her/my life. Please forgive all generational sin, and any place where fear or torment was passed through the bloodline. I/We apply the precious blood of Jesus to heal all unresolved grief and pain.

I/We speak to my/name's conscious memory, unconscious memory, and subconscious memory, and command all trauma, fear, shock, pain, and shame to be removed by the power of the Holy Spirit. I/We speak to the amygdala, and remove all trauma from the emotions. Lord, I/we ask that You turn off all "fear alarms" that have been ringing. Let Godly discernment replace the fear that has acted as a guard. I/We speak to the immune system and command all toxins and hormones to be released and come into proper alignment. Lord, I/we ask that you wash over my/name's eyes and ears, and remove the trauma from all images and sounds that have hurt them. Lord, remove any trauma or shame associated with scent and remove all trauma from the skin. Let all trauma be removed from my/name's will and emotions. Let all trauma be removed from the muscles, ligaments, tendons, bones, and bone marrow. Let all trauma be removed from the organs of my/name's body. (Ask the Lord for any specific organs to pray for.) Lord, I/we break all fear bonds, trauma bonds, and unhealthy and unholy soul ties that have been created through trauma, in the name of Jesus.

Lord, I/we invite you to sing over me/name, bring everything in him/her/me into alignment with Your song for him/her/me. In the name of Jesus, I prophecy order and healing into your/my spirit, soul, and body. Fill every cell with peace and healing, Jesus. Let Your light displace all darkness. Send Your angels to guard me/name, and let him/her/me experience Your love and presence. Amen.

UNGODLY BELIEFS PRAYER

For use with the Ungodly Beliefs Worksheet in part 3.

1. I confess my sin and my ancestor's sin of believing the lie that _____.

2. I forgive those who contributed to my forming this lie.

3. I ask You, Lord, to forgive me for receiving this lie, for living my life based on it, and for anyway I have judged others because of it. I receive Your forgiveness.

4. On the basis of Your forgiveness, Lord, I choose to forgive myself for believing this lie.

5. I renounce and break my agreement with this lie. I break my agreement with the power of darkness. I cancel all agreements I may have made with demons.

6. I choose to accept, believe, and receive the truth that _____.

Acknowledgment for this prayer is given to Chester and Betsy Kylstra, Proclaiming His Word Publishing, 2849 Laurel Park Highway, Hendersonville, NC 28739, (828) 696-9075, office@restoringthefoundations.org/restoringthefoundations.org. Used by permission. Minor changes incorporated by Healing Hearts International Ministries, 2023.

VOWS/JUDGMENTS PRAYER

Ministry steps for Curses (Vows or Judgments) spoken by you to others.

I ask You to forgive me, Lord, for speaking this curse (vow or judgment) against _____.

I forgive myself for speaking this curse (vow or judgment).

I remove all legal rights and powers I gave to the demonic to carry out this curse (vow or judgment).

I release God's freedom and healing to _____.

Ministry steps for Curses (Vows or Judgments) spoken by others/self to you.

I forgive _____ for cursing me with the spoken word that _____.

I ask You to forgive me, Lord, for receiving this curse and giving it a place in my life.

I break the legal rights and powers of this curse in my life, based on the shed blood of Jesus Christ and His finished work on the Cross. I am no longer in agreement in any way with this curse. I appropriate the power of the Cross to stop all judgements and demons associated with this curse.

I receive God's freedom from the effects of this word curse. I affirm that God's blessings are active in my life, and not curses. I receive _____.

Prayers used by permission from Restoring the Foundations Ministries, www.RestoringTheFoundations.org.

PART TWO:

DELIVERANCE

DELIVERANCE PRAYER

Dear Lord Jesus, I believe that You are the Son of God. I believe that You died on the cross for my sins and that You rose again from the dead, and you are at the right hand of the Father.

I accept you, and confess You as my Lord and my Savior. I repent and renounce, and ask your forgiveness for every sin that I have committed, spoken, or thought in rebellion, disobedience, weakness, or in ignorance.

I repent of and renounce, every sinful word I have ever spoken or thought about you God. I break all curses on me or my family due to blasphemy or cursing You, by me, my family or prior generations. I repent of and renounce every sinful thought or word against any servant of Yours. I repent for having lifted my hands against Your anointed ones. I repent of and renounce every sinful word I have spoken, or thought about my parents, and any act that I committed that dishonored my father or mother. I break every vow and every judgment I have placed on my mother and father, for whatever they did, or did not do. I now break; I NOW BREAK all curses brought on me by these sins.

I renounce all curses on me handed down by my family or prior generations. I do not choose to practice any sins of my parents or my ancestors. I forgive my parents and ancestors for causing any curse to come upon me.

I repent of all my contacts with Satan and all his evil works. I renounce all involvement with witchcraft and the occult. I repent of, and renounce all demon spirits that I have allowed to enter my life.

Lord, I forgive all others who have wronged me or harmed me. I lay down all resentment, all bitterness, all hatred, and all rebellion. In particular, I forgive _____ (name them and give them to the Lord).

Lord Jesus, I ask You to forgive me and to cleanse me by Your precious Blood. I accept it now. I accept Your forgiveness and I forgive myself.

Satan, because of the blood, you have no power over me, and you have no place in me. I now cancel any legal right you claim to remain. In the Mighty Name of Jesus, Amen!

Lord, You have said, whosoever shall call on the Name of the Lord, shall be delivered. I call on your name right now, and I recognize you as my deliverer.

Now, Lord, I loose myself from every demon spirit that I have allowed to influence my life, in the Name of Jesus, and I command them to leave me now, touching or harming no one. In the Name of Jesus, Amen!

Acknowledgment is given to Teresa Castleman's book "Brownsville Deliverance Maunal" 1996-97

STRONGHOLD OF ANTI-CHRIST

1 John 4:3

I renounce the stronghold of antichrist and every spirit of antichrist, and its manifestations & fruit.

I renounce

- Any spirit that:
  - Denies the deity of Christ
  - Denies the atonement
  - Comes against Christ and His teaching
  - Suppresses ministries
- Secular humanism
- Jezebel
- Worldly speech & actions
- Profanity
- Antichristian
- Lawlessness
- The Accuser
- The Deceiver
- Any serpent spirit
- Mermaid Spirit
- Python Spirit
- Kundalini Spirit
- Anger towards God

- An antichrist spirit that comes in through rock music, rap music, or any ungodly music, and break all programming from music, at every level of the mind
- Legalism, ritualism, or formalism
- Idolatry
- A Religious Spirit
- Teachers of heresies
  - Mormonism
  - Catholicism
  - Phariseeism
  - Unitarianism
  - Nazism
  - Communism
  - Buddhism
  - Hinduism
  - New Age
  - Freemasonry
  - Islam
- Familiar spirit and generational Spirit of antichrist

STRONGHOLD OF BONDAGE

Romans 8:15

I renounce the stronghold of bondage and its manifestations and fruit.

I renounce:

- Bondage to fear
- Bondage to all addictions:
    - Drugs
    - Alcohol
    - Cigarettes
    - Exercise /gym culture
    - Food/diet lifestyles
    - Sex
    - Pornography
    - Masturbation
    - T.V., movies, videos, games, tablets
    - Computers, phones, internet
    - Shopping
    - Gambling
    - Social media
- Bondage to lust or perversion
- A Bound spirit
- A Mind-binding spirit
- Bondage to sin
- Bondage to rejection and self hate
- Compulsive behavior
- Compulsive sin
- Captivity to Satan
- Servant to corruption
- Religious bondage
- Religious tradition
- Traditions of men
- Idolatry
- Bondage to ambition and achievement
- Bondage to bitterness and unforgiveness
- Bondage to oppression
- Spiritual blindness and deafness
- Fear of death
- Spiritual death
- Control
- Insecurity
- Accusations
- Injustice
- Familiar spirit and generational spirit of bondage

STRONGHOLD OF A DEAF & DUMB SPIRIT

Mark 9:25

I renounce the deaf and dumb spirit, and its manifestations & fruit.

I renounce:

- Dumb and mute
- Deafness and spiritual deafness
- Blindness and spiritual blindness
- Injuries involving drowning or burning
- Compulsive behavior
- Mental illness
- Madness
- Insanity
- Retardation
- Senility
- Schizophrenia
- Paranoia
- Hearing voices
- Hallucinations
- Palsy
- ADD, ADHD, Learning disorders
- D.I.D./M.P.D.
- Crippling

- Crying and tearing
- Ear problems
- Foaming at the mouth
- Alzheimer's Disease
- Gnashing of teeth
- Pining away
- Prostration
- Suicidal
- Chemical imbalance – Bi-polar
- Seizures & Epilepsy
- Self-hatred
- Self-mutilation and self- punishment
- Eating disorders
- A Zombie spirit
- Double mindedness
- Familiar spirit and generational spirit of deaf & dumb

STRONGHOLD OF DEATH

1 Corinthians 15:26

I renounce the spirit of death and the curse of premature death.

I break all plans of the enemy, past, present, and future, and I break every assignment against my life due to:

- Accidents
- Assault
- Abduction
- Injury
- Illness
- Infirmity
- Random acts of violence
- Disease
- Cancer
- Suicide
- Clumsiness
- Fighting
- Dare devil acts
- Speeding
- Murder
- HIV/AIDS
- Hepatitis C

I break every assignment of:

- Abortion
- Miscarriages
- Death
- Destruction
- Delay

And I break every assignment of death to my:

- Ministry and calling
- Anointing and spiritual gifts
- Relationships
- Marriage
- Family
- Emotions
- Finances
- Dreams
- And I renounce the familiar spirit and generational spirit of death

STRONGHOLD OF DIVINATION

Acts 16:16

I renounce the stronghold of divination, the occult and witchcraft, and its manifestations and fruit.

I renounce:

- Lust for power and control
- Fortune teller, soothsayer, and psychics
- Water Spirits
- Self-will
- Stargazer, zodiac, and horoscopes
- False prophets
- Warlock, witch, sorcerer, and wizard
- Mind-control
- Manipulation and control
- Automatic handwriting and handwriting analysis
- Shaman and witchdoctor
- All spirit guides
- All animal guides
- All Indian witchcraft
- Astral projection
- Druid and Celtic witchcraft
- Occultism and syncretism
- Rebellion
- Hypnotist, and enchanter
- Acupuncture
- Drug use, illegal or prescription
- Birth charts
- All magic, black or white
- A Serpent spirit
- A Vampire spirit
- A Mermaid spirit
- Spiritist
- Jezebel
- Water witching and divination
- WICCA
- Numerology and Reflexology
- Yoga/Kundalini
- Harry Potter
- Voodoo and Santeria/Brujeria
- Imaginary friends
- Island witchcraft
- Gypsy
- Satanism/luciferianism
- Superstitions and Old Wives Tales
- Charms
- Fascination with evil
- Charismatic witchcraft
- Demonic movies, games, books, and music
- Freemasonry
- Martial arts
- Tattoos and piercing
- Familiar spirit and generational spirit of divination & witchcraft

STRONGHOLD OF ERROR

1 John 4:6

I renounce the stronghold of error and its manifestation and fruit.

I renounce:

- A spirit of error
- All false prophecies spoken over me by anyone, including myself
- Un-submissive/dishonor
- Hyper-spiritual
- Hypocrisy
- All false doctrines
  - Mormonism
  - Catholicism/Jesuit
  - Pharisism
  - Buddhism
  - Hinduism
  - New Age movement
  - Unitarianism
  - Communism
  - Nazism
  - Freemasonry
  - Islam
- Twisting Scripture
- An un-teachable spirit
- Mixing the holy with the profane

- A defensive and argumentative spirit
- Sympathy for the devil
- Contentions
- Servant of corruption
- Having a form of godliness but denying its power
- Mental confusion and fears
- Physical illness, pain and affliction
- Depression and suicidal
- Dullness of comprehension
- Spiritual hindrances to:
  - Prayer
  - Bible study
  - Listening to services
  - Moving in the gifts of the Spirit
- All faith principles that have come in through error
- Familiar spirit and generational spirit of error

STRONGHOLD OF A FAMILIAR SPIRIT

Leviticus 19:31

I renounce all familiar spirits, all knowing spirits, and generational spirits, and their manifestations & fruit.

I renounce the familiar spirit of:

- Fear
- Death
- Anti-Christ
- Religion
- Bondage
- Haughtiness
- Heaviness
- Whoredoms
- Seducing and enticing
- Deaf and Dumb
- Jealousy
- Perverse and incest
- Homosexuality
- Lying
- Infirmity
- Divination
- Error
- Rejection
- Inferiority and low self-esteem
- Bigotry & racism

- Self-pity
- Divorce
- Abortion
- Slavery
- Poverty and lack

I also renounce:

- Necromancer
- Medium and wizard
- Yoga and all mantras
- Chants and spells
- Clairvoyant
- Spiritist
- Passive mind-dreamers
- Spirit guides & animal guides
- All false prophecies
- Drug use
- The deceiver and the accuser
- The Tormentor
- Illegitimacy

STRONGHOLD OF FEAR

ll Timothy 1:7

I renounce the stronghold of fear, and its manifestations and fruit.

I renounce:

- A spirit of fear
- A Critical spirit
- Untrusting & Doubt
- Worry and Unbelief
- Anxiety and Stress
- Panic attacks
- Migraines
- Torment & Horror
- Terror and Nightmares
- Fear of the dark
- Fear of death
  - Death to self
  - Death to family
- Hermit and recluse
- Introvert
- An alone spirit
- Fear of man
- Fear of men
- Fear of women
- Fear of commitment
- Fear of relationships
- Fear of molestation or rape
- Fear of rejection
- Fear of abandonment
- Self provision
- Self protection
- Extrovert
- Heart attack and fear of heart attack
- Fear of abuse
- Fear of authority
- Fear of saying no
- Fear of failure
- Fear of the future
- Perfectionist
- Not good enough
- Fear of food
- Unhealthy fear of God
- All Phobias
  - Heights
  - Animals
  - Spiders
  - Water, etc.
- Fear that came in from horror movies
- Fear of embarrassment
- Fear of shame
- Fear of public speaking
- Fear of lack
- Fear of conflict
- Fear of not having fear
- Familiar spirit and generational spirit of fear

STRONGHOLD OF HAUGHTINESS

Proverbs 16:18

I renounce the stronghold of haughtiness, and its manifestations & fruit.

I renounce:

- Arrogant and smug
- Vain and vanity
- All Pride
- Rationalization in the area of pride
- Professional pride
- National pride
- Regional pride
- Religious pride
- Bragging and boastful
- Egotistical
- Scornful
- Obstinate
- Self-righteous
- Dictatorial and controlling
- Overbearing and domineering
- Manipulation and control
- Rejection of God and rejection of authority
- All Rebellion
- False humility
- A Holier than thou attitude
- Exalted feelings
- Narcissist
- Gossip
- Division
- Dissention
- Contentious
- Strife
- Self-deception and self-delusion
- Idleness
- Performer
- Attention seeker and demonstrative
- Interruption
- Impatience
- Always right
- Critical and fault finding
- Leviathan
- Haughtiness that came in through abuse and hurts
- Familiar spirit and generational spirit of haughtiness

STRONGHOLD OF HEAVINESS

Isaiah 61:3

I renounce the stronghold of heaviness and its manifestations and fruit.

I renounce:

- Sorrow and grief
- Self-pity
- Embarrassment
- Shame
- Injustice
- A broken heart
- Inner hurts and a torn spirit
- Regrets from the unfairness of life
- Excessive mourning
- False responsibility
- Suicidal thoughts
- Gluttony, bulimia and anorexia
- Loneliness
- Heaviness and depression
- Discouragement and despair
- Dejection and hopelessness
- Inferiority and low self-esteem
- Lack of praise & unpacified emotions
- Suppressed emotions: fear, anger, rage, violence, hatred
- Self-hate
- Self-mutilation and self-punishment
- Insomnia
- Chemical imbalance
- Rejection - insecurity & abandonment - see Root of Rejection on next page
- Familiar spirit and generational spirit of heaviness

STRONGHOLD OF REJECTION

Isaiah 61: 3

I renounce the spirit of rejection that entered:

- While in the womb
- During childbirth (through trauma or by not being the gender parents wanted)
- While in a hospital
- By not bonding with mother at birth
- By not bonding with my father
- Through adoption or the threat of adoption
- Through childhood hurts and abuse at home or at school
- Thought hurts and abuse at church
- Through separation or divorce or the threat of divorce
- Through death of a loved one
- By betrayal or a broken engagement
- By loss of a job
- Through depression
- Through perceived or expected rejection
- Through guilt or shame
- Through actual abandonment and rejection
- Through a familiar spirit and generational spirit of rejection

STRONGHOLD OF INFIRMITY

Luke 13:11

I renounce the stronghold of infirmity, and its manifestations & fruit; And I break every assignment: past, present, and future

I renounce:

- Hypochondria
- A bent body and spine
- Neck and back problems
- Chemical imbalance
- Hormone imbalance
- High fever
- All mental illness
- Bi-polar
- Impotent – frail and lame
- Arthritis and a root of bitterness
- Diabetes
- All oppression
- Pain and affliction
- All lingering disorders
- Migraines
- TB & Emphysema
- Fibromyalgia
- Lyme disease
- Blood disorders
- Female problems
- Alzheimer's and dementia
- Scoliosis
- All depression
- Cancer
- Tumors, cysts and growths
- Weakness, tiredness and fatigue
- All infections, viral, bacterial, fungal, strep and staph
- Asthma, allergies and hay fever
- Epilepsy and seizures
- Auto Immune
- Sexually transmitted diseases
- Parasites
- Fear of infirmity, sickness and disease
- Familiar spirit and generational spirit of infirmity, sickness and disease

STRONGHOLD OF JEALOUSY

Proverbs 6:34

I renounce the stronghold of jealousy, and its manifestation and fruit.

I renounce:

- Jealousy
- Murder
- Revenge and spite
- Cruelty
- Extreme competition
- Causing divisions
- Coveting
- Selfishness
- Envy
- Strife
- Contention
- Frustration
- Hatred

- Anger and rage
- Violence
- Bigotry and racism
- Abuse and abuser
- A Vigilante spirit
- Passive aggressive
- Suppressed anger and rage
- Exalted feelings/haughtiness/pride
- Familiar spirit and generational spirit of jealousy

STRONGHOLD OF LYING

II Chronicles 18:22

I renounce the stronghold of lying, and its manifestations & fruit.

I renounce:

- Strong deception
- Self-deception
- And break all false prophecies, and the power of the words spoken over me
- Gossip
- Flattery
- Exaggeration
- False memories
- All lies I have believed about myself
- The lie that I'll never be free
- Lies from false teachers
- All lies – white & black
- Slander
- Accusations
- Religious bondages
- Superstitions and old wives tales
- Profanity
- Guilt, shame and condemnation
- Homosexual, bisexual, transgender, pansexual, non-binary, and lesbian
- Melancholy spirit
- False burdens
- Driving zeal
- Covenant breaker
- Frenzied emotional actions
- A split tongue
- Familiar spirit and generational spirit of lying

STRONGHOLD OF PERVERSE

Isaiah 19:14

I renounce the stronghold of perverse, and its manifestations & fruit.

I renounce:

- Lying
- A Broken spirit
- Uncleanness & lewdness
- Illegitimacy
- Evil actions
- Abortion
- Child abuse & molestation
- Incest – physical & emotional
- Prostitution – body, soul, spirit
- Masturbation and self-gratification
- Exposure and voyeurism
- Atheist
- A filthy mind
- Sex perversions
- Orgies
- Doctrinal error
- Twisting the word
- Satanic ritual abuse
- Ritual molestation and rape
- Satanic dedications and marriage ceremonies
- Rape
- Sodomy

- Pornography
- Chronic worrier
- Self-lover and narcissist
- Egocentric thinking
- Contentious and foolish
- Lust
- Homosexual and lesbianism
- Bisexual/bestiality/pansexuality/a-sexuality/ furries
- Bisexual and bestiality
- S & M (Sadomasochism)
- Vain imagination and fantasy lust
- Frigid spirit (sexual or emotional)
- Effeminate spirit (males only)
- Masculine spirit (females only)
- Fornication and adultery
- All sexual demons, inc.
  - Incubus
  - Succubus
  - Lillith
- Familiar spirit and generational spirit of perverse

STRONGHOLD OF SEDUCING SPIRITS

1 Timothy 4:1

I renounce the stronghold of seducing and deceiving spirits, and their manifestations and fruit.

I renounce:

- A seared conscience
- All deception
- A vigilante spirit
- All fascination to:
  - Evil ways
  - Evil objects
  - Evil persons
  - Evil images
- Seducers and enticers
- Flirtation
- Wandering from the truth
- Hypocritical lies
- Double standards
- Ambush
- Setup
- Being a target/gullible

- All attraction to and fascination with:
  - False prophets
  - False signs & wonders
  - Demonic movies, videos and games
  - Demonic and sexual books
  - Sexual movies, videos and games
- Pornography
- A Jezebel spirit
- An Ahab spirit
- Familiar spirit and generational spirit of Seducers and Enticers

STRONGHOLD OF WHOREDOMS

Hosea 5:4

I renounce the stronghold of prostitution and whoredoms, and its manifestations & fruit.

I renounce:

- All unfaithfulness
- Adultery
- Fornication
- Harlotry
- Prostitution – Spirit, Soul, Body
- Love of money
- Materialism
- Love of control
- Love of power
- Excessive appetites
- Worldliness/finding identity in worldly culture
- Worldly speech and actions
- Idolatry
- Baal/Bel worship
- Pornography
- Chronic dissatisfaction
- Love of self
- Self- reward
- Familiar spirit and generational spirit of Whoredoms

SEALING PRAYER

Blessing - pray over client following deliverance sessions

May the Lord bless you and keep you; may His face shine upon you and give you peace (Numbers 6:24-26). You are fearfully and wonderfully made, His masterpiece, created for good works in Christ Jesus (Psalm 139:14, Ephesians 2:10). May you walk in the freedom for which Christ has set you free, standing firm and not letting anything entangle you again (Galatians 5:1). Be strong and courageous, for the Lord your God is with you wherever you go (Joshua 1:9). We declare that His Spirit within you is greater than anything in the world (1 John 4:4), and that His power is made perfect in your weakness (2 Corinthians 12:9). Step boldly into the identity He has given you, knowing that He has plans to prosper you and give you hope and a future (Jeremiah 29:11). You are loved with an everlasting love, and nothing can separate you from it (Jeremiah 31:3, Romans 8:38-39). May His joy be your strength and His peace guard your heart and mind as you move forward in His purpose for your life (Nehemiah 8:10, Philippians 4:7).

Sealing Prayer - used to close a session, or for the client to pray at home

In the name of Jesus, we command every spirit released in this place to go directly to the feet of Jesus, because all of His enemies will be made His footstool. (Ps 110:1) You cannot attach to or follow_____ (client) or any of us praying today. We bind and forbid any retaliation, retribution, harassment or punishment to come against any of us, the ministry, our families, or anything connected to us in the powerful name of Jesus. We seal the work that was done today with the Blood of Jesus. Thank you Lord for the promise in Ps 91, that says when we make the most High our refuge, we live under the shadow of Your wings. We claim that promise for ourselves and all that concerns us today. Thank you Lord, for all that You accomplished today in _____'s life. We give you all the glory and the honor for the healing and deliverance he/she has received. In the powerful name of Jesus, Amen!

DELIVERANCE SESSION REPORT

CONFIDENTIAL INFORMATION

Personal Ministry

Deliverance Session Report

Name: _____ Place of Ministry: _____

Date: _____ Hours Worked: _____

Deliverance Team Leader: _____

Ministering Team Members: _____

_____,_____,_____

_____,_____,_____

Strongholds dealt with in this session:

❑ Anti-Christ   ❑ Fear   ❑ Perverse

❑ Bondage   ❑ Haughtiness   ❑ Seducing

❑ Deaf & Dumb   ❑ Heaviness   ❑ Whoredoms

❑ Death   ❑ Infirmity   ❑ Masonic

❑ Divination   ❑ Jealousy   ❑ Other

❑ Error   ❑ Rejection

❑ Familiar Spirit   ❑ Lying

Comments:

_____

_____

_____

_____

PART THREE:

TEACHING TOOLS

UNGODLY BELIEFS WORKSHEET

Read the following statements, and check the ones that you feel, not what you think you know. Ask the Holy Spirit to show you other ungodly beliefs that you may have. (By the way, all of us have ungodly beliefs!)

Theme: Rejection, Not Belonging

_____1. I don't belong, I will always be on the outside (left out).

_____2. My feelings don't count. No one cares what I feel.

_____3. No one will love me or care about me just for myself.

_____4. I will always be lonely. The special man (woman) in my life will not be there for me.

_____5. I will isolate myself so that I won't be vulnerable to hurt, rejection, etc. anymore.

_____6. _____

Theme: Unworthiness, Guilt, Shame

_____1. I am not worthy to receive anything from God.

_____2. I am the problem. When something is wrong, it is my fault.

_____3. I am a bad person. If you knew the real me, you would reject me.

_____4. I must wear a mask so that people won't find out how horrible I am and reject me.

_____5. I have messed up so badly that I have missed God's best for me.

_____6. _____

Theme: Doing to achieve Self-Worth, Value, Recognition

_____1. I will never get credit for what I do.

_____2. My value is in what I do. I am valuable because I do good to others, because I am "successful."

_____3. Even when I do/give my best, it is not good enough. I can never meet the standard.

_____4. I will choose to be passive in order to avoid conflict that would risk others' disapproval.

_____5. God doesn't care if I have a "secret life," as long as I appear to be good.

_____6. _____

Theme: Control (to avoid hurt)

____1. I have to plan every day of my life. I have to continually plan/strategize. I can't relax.

____2. The perfect life is one in which no conflict is allowed, and so there is peace.

____3. _____

Theme: Physical

____1. I am unattractive. God short-changed me.

____2. I am doomed to have certain physical disabilities. They are just part of what I have inherited.

____3. It is impossible to lose weight (or gain weight). I am just stuck.

____4. I am not competent /complete as a man (woman).

____5. _____

Theme: Personality Traits

____1. I will always be (angry, shy, jealous, insecure, fearful, etc.)

____2. _____

Theme: Identity

____1. I should have been a boy (girl). Then my parents would have valued/loved me more,….. etc.

____2. Men (women) have it better.

____3. I will never be known or appreciated for my real self.

____4. I will never really change and be as God wants me to be.

____5._____

Theme: Miscellaneous

____1. I have wasted a lot of time and energy, some of my best years.

____2. Turmoil is normal for me.

____3. I will always have financial problems.

____4. _____

UNGODLY BELIEFS ABOUT OTHERS

Read the following statements, and check the ones that you feel, not what you think you know.

Theme: Safety/Protection

_____1. I must be very guarded about what I say, since anything I say may be used against me.

_____2. I have to guard and hide my emotions and feelings; I cannot give anyone the satisfaction of knowing that they have wounded or hurt me. I'll not be vulnerable, humiliated, or shamed.

_____3.

_____

_____4.

_____

Theme: Retaliation

_____1. The correct way to respond if someone offends me is to punish them by withdrawing, and / or cutting them off.

_____2. I will make sure that _____ hurts as much as I hurt!

_____3.

_____

Theme: Victim

_____1. Authority figures will humiliate me and violate me.

_____2. Others will just use and abuse me.

_____3. My value is based totally on others' judgment / perception about me.

_____4. I am completely under their authority. I have no will or choice of my own.

_____5. I will not be known, understood, loved, or appreciated for who I am by those close to me.

_____6.

_____

_____7.

_____

Theme: Hopelessness / Helplessness

____1. I am out there all alone. If I get into trouble or need help, there is no one to rescue me.

____2. _____

____3. _____

Theme: Defective in Relationships

____1. I will never be able to fully give or receive love. I don't know what it is.

____2. If I let anyone get close to me, I may get my heart broken again. I can't let myself risk it.

____3. If I fail to please you, I won't receive your pleasure and acceptance of me. Therefore, I must strive even more (perfectionism). I must do whatever is necessary to try to please you.

____4. _____

____5. _____

Theme: God

____1. God loves other people more than He loves me.

____2. God only values me for what I do. My life is just a means to an end.

____3. No matter how much I try, I'll never be able to do enough or do it well enough to please God.

____4. God is judging me when I relax. I have to stay busy with His work or He will abandon me.

____5. God has let me down before; He may do it again. I can't trust Him, or feel secure with Him.

____6. _____

SOUL TIES

Breaking Ungodly Soul Ties

Understanding and breaking ungodly soul ties can be a major key to freedom! You can have a soul tie with a person, a place, or a thing. There are sexual soul ties and/or emotional soul ties. The Bible talks about sexual soul ties in 1 Corinthians 6:16, "Or do you not know that he who is joined to a harlot is one body with her? For "the two," He says, "shall become one flesh." A good illustration of what happens with a soul tie is if you were to glue two pieces of paper together. When you rip them apart, a little of each paper will be attached to the other. We are asking the Lord to clean up the separation; to call back every part of our soul attached to them and send back every part of their soul attached to us.

Genesis 34:1-3 provides another example of a sexual soul tie, "Now Dinah daughter of Leah, whom she bore to Jacob, went out [unattended] to see the girls of the place. And when Shechem son of Hamor the Hivite, prince of the country, saw her, he seized her, lay with her, and humbled, defiled, and disgraced her. But his soul longed for and clung to Dinah daughter of Jacob, and he loved the girl and spoke comfortingly to her young heart's wishes."

Whenever someone has sex outside of a marriage covenant, even through abuse, a sexual soul tie is formed and needs to be broken!

There are also emotional soul ties, both good and bad. 1 Samuel 18:1 gives us an example of a good emotional soul tie. "When David had finished speaking to Saul, the soul of Jonathan was knit with the soul of David, and Jonathan loved him as his own life." Examples of ungodly emotional soul ties would be relationships that feel draining or toxic. Emotional soul ties can be with parents, siblings, close friends, spiritual leaders, etc.

Emotional soul ties are also possible with places or things. An example of a soul tie to a place would be moving to a new state but constantly talking or thinking about your old house or city. It can also be places like a former church, Grandma's house, or a place where you experienced abuse. Soul ties to objects can be family heirlooms, love letters or gifts from former romantic relationships, freemasonry regalia handed down to you, or even habits like pornography or smoking.

People often find when they break ungodly soul ties, they are able to move on from relationships, let go of past events and experiences, and get rid of objects the Holy Spirit is asking them to throw out.

Use Soul Ties prayer for ministry to soul ties.

STEPS FOR INNER HEALING

These are tools to lead someone through Inner Healing. Holy Spirit can change the order or add things, don't be restricted by these steps, but use them as a guide.

The steps can be used for children and adults.

1. Ask client to close their eyes, say "Jesus, I give you permission to heal my heart, and I give myself permission to be healed. Jesus, please take me to any memory that You would like to heal today."

2. Encourage them to describe what they remember or what they see. Normally this will be a trauma. Remind them, do not second guess yourself, trust yourself, trust God.

3. When they see a memory, have them ask, "Jesus, who do I need to forgive in this memory?" Walk them through looking at the person in the memory, and telling them what they did and how they felt, and then saying, "I choose to forgive you and release you to Jesus." This may include forgiving themselves and releasing God. Oftentimes, when they cannot see Jesus after forgiveness, they either need to forgive themselves or God.

4. When forgiveness is done, have them invite Jesus into the memory, "Jesus, would you come into this memory, heal my heart, and show me truth?"

5. When they see or sense Jesus, ask them to describe where He is and what He's doing. Have them walk to Him.

6. Have them ask, "Jesus, what lie did I believe in this memory?" Remind them to listen for His voice.

7. Have them ask, "Jesus, what's the truth?"

8. Have them say, "Jesus, I give You permission to remove everything that attached to me, and heal my heart."

9. Check in and ask what Jesus is doing, (to make sure there is no interference and what is happening is positive.) They should start to feel peace as He ministers to them.

10. Encourage them to stay with Jesus until He is all finished and they feel peace.

11. If needed, have them ask God to take them to the next memory He wants to heal.

HEALING AFTER ABORTION

Step 1: The Invitation for Self-Forgiveness

- Guidance: Invite the client to close her eyes in a quiet, comfortable space.

- Action: Gently guide her to forgive herself for having an abortion. This is a crucial step in the healing process, acknowledging her feelings and experiences with compassion.

Step 2: Repentance and Reconciliation

- Guidance: Lead the client in a prayer of repentance, turning towards the Lord for forgiveness and healing.

- Action: Guide the client through a heartfelt conversation with God, expressing remorse and seeking and receiving His loving forgiveness.

Step 3: Forgiving Others

- Guidance: Encourage the client to extend forgiveness to everyone involved in the abortion experience. This includes the father, doctors, and even God, for any feelings of abandonment or anger.

- Action: Help the client articulate her forgiveness, releasing any bitterness or resentment, and embracing forgiveness.

Step 4: Inviting the Holy Spirit's Healing

- Guidance: Open the space for the Holy Spirit to bring healing and comfort. This is a moment of surrender and trust in the divine process.

- Action: Lead the client in a prayer, giving the Holy Spirit permission to heal her heart and mind.

Step 5: Discovering the Unseen Bond

- Guidance: Assist the client in connecting with her unborn child through the Holy Spirit. This step is about acknowledging and honoring the life that was.

- Action: Ask the Holy Spirit to reveal the gender of the baby, and the baby's name, and middle name.

Step 6: A Moment of Connection

- Guidance: Allow time for the client to hold her baby in this Inner Healing space. Encourage her to express any unspoken words, emotions, or love to her child.

- Action: Guide her through this emotional release, allowing her to communicate anything she wishes to her baby.

Step 7: Entrusting the Child to Jesus

- Guidance: Lead the client in the act of entrusting her baby to Jesus. This step is about letting go and knowing that Jesus is caring for her child.

- Action: Encourage her to ask Jesus to watch over her baby until they can be reunited in heaven, handing over her child to His care.

Step 8: Action

- Guidance: Recognize that the abortion experience might have multiple memories that need to be addressed with inner healing.

- Action: Ask the Holy Spirit to take her to any other specific memories or trauma that need to be addressed and healed as part of this journey.

See Steps for Inner Healing for Ministry Steps

Suggested Deliverance Strongholds - these or others may need to be addressed, as Holy Spirit leads

- Death - may come into the womb

- Fear, heaviness, perversion, etc.

Note: These ministry steps may be adapted for use with other family members (father of the baby, the woman's mother, etc.) as needed. These steps are also very effective when adapted for miscarriage healing.

SONSHIP TEACHING

1 John 3:1a - Behold what manner of love the Father has bestowed on us, that we should be called children of God!

John 1:12 - But as many as received Him, to them He gave the right to become children of God.

Gal 3:26 - For you are all sons of God through faith in Christ Jesus.

We all have been adopted into the family of God, but there are places of trauma, disappointment, brokenness, pain, or hurt in our past. For most people, these things caused us at some point to not trust the authority over us, caused you to want to protect yourself. Out of wanting to protect yourself, you say, "Never again, I can't trust anyone, I can only trust myself." In that pain, you let go of your sonship, let go of allowing yourself to be a son or daughter, therefore taking the responsibility to protect your own heart. When this happens, we can take on an orphan spirit, and/or a slave mentality. Many of us have both!

What does an Orphan Spirit and a Slave Mentality sound like?

Orphan spirit: I'm on my own, I have no one, I have to protect myself, no one will help, it's all up to me

Slave mentality: I have to earn love. I will work as hard as I have to; to prove I'm worthy of loving. I will work until you recognize and care about me.

This is the prayer we'll use to break the Orphan Spirit and the Slave Mentality, and allow God to heal the trauma. Let God move you into position with a healed heart. Understanding Sonship teaches us how to walk our relationship with God, to receive all He has for you.

Use Sonship Prayer for Ministry on this subject.

FORGIVENESS HOMEWORK

Without the power of forgiveness, you have no freedom.

Matthew 18:34-35 says, "And his master was angry and delivered him to the torturers until he should pay all that was due to him, so my heavenly Father also will do to you if each of you, from his heart, does not forgive his brother his trespasses."

Webster's dictionary defines torture as: "Extreme pain, anguish of **body or mind, pain, agony or torment**. Torment to put to extreme pain and misery, either body or mind." The tormentors or torturers are demon spirits. They have a legal right to torment you if you have unforgiveness. When we plant unforgiveness, bitterness will spring up. **Bitterness has been defined as unfulfilled revenge.**

When someone hurts us, the pain is real. The hurt is real. Unforgiveness is like being in prison or in chains. Assume you could see into the spirit realm; whoever has hurt you and you have not forgiven them, there are chains attached to their ankle and to yours. You are bound to each other. They can continue to hurt you for the rest of your life, because every time the hurt replays in your mind, up comes the pain.

Unforgiveness can also build a wall around your heart that you believe can protect you from being hurt. However, instead of that wall protecting you, it becomes a prison. You won't let anyone on the inside of that wall, that includes the Holy Spirit. In this prison, all your pain is also trapped within these walls. The pain cannot get out, and you cease to be able to feel, your emotions become flatlined.

Let me explain what true forgiveness is, and is not. Forgiveness is NOT saying what a person did to you is okay. It is not okay and it will never be okay. It was wrong. Forgiveness is NOT a feeling; it is obedience to God's Word. Forgiveness is NOT healing; **it paves the way or opens the door for healing**. If you have forgiven someone and still feel pain, it's because you need to receive healing. The forgiveness comes first, then the healing.

Forgiveness IS a sin issue - it is commanded in Scripture to forgive. It is not a choice.

Matthew 6:14-15 says, "For if you forgive men their trespasses, your heavenly Father will also forgive you. But if you do not forgive their trespasses, neither will your Father forgive your trespasses."

We have to understand we have no right to hold anyone in unforgiveness. And this includes forgiving yourself! You must forgive yourself. It also includes God. If you blame God or there is hurt towards God, you need to release Him. Forgiveness IS NOT a choice.

It IS a decision with your will, to obey God, and to trust Him with your hurt. Forgiveness is releasing the person to God.

1 John 1:9 says, "If we confess our sins, he is faithful and just and will forgive us our sins and purify us from all unrighteousness." Acknowledge to God what emotions this wrong produced in you, choose to forgive and release them to God. Then you can be healed and purified.

FORGIVENESS WORK

You will need a pen and paper.

1. Get alone and ask the Lord to show you the people you need to forgive.

2. Write down names of people you need to forgive, make a list. (This can include family, bullies, teachers, kids at school, ex's, abuse, etc.) Be sure you include yourself, and God.

3. Go over each name with the Lord and express to Him how they have hurt you. For each name the Lord gave you, write a letter. You do not mail these letters, you can tear them up, throw them away, it's up to you. This is just for your healing; nobody has to see them.

4. Write down what they did and how they made you feel, until all the emotion and hurt from that person is out on the page. (Example: The girl in fifth grade, made fun of me, embarrassed me in front of everyone, made me feel worthless, I felt angry, scared, rejected, hopeless, etc.)

5. Once you feel you've gotten all emotion of the hurt onto the page, choose to forgive and release them. Say "Lord, I choose to forgive and release (name the person)."

We talked about forgiving ourselves. This step is very important, but may be the hardest. Get some tissues and go somewhere alone, the bathroom, or your bedroom with a mirror. Look at yourself in the mirror, forgive and release yourself for each thing. After you forgive yourself, look in the mirror and begin to speak over yourself the truth about who you are, not how you feel, but what God says about you. And say, "I receive," when you're done.

BREAKTHROUGH CONNECTIONS

This is a tool to bring breakthrough in conversations, to bring understanding of both people's hearts, and to make an action plan to move forward in a new way. Learning to communicate is key in all relationships and gives God room to work.

The one rule is, if you are asking the questions, you cannot comment, explain, defend, or blame. You must simply listen to understand the heart of the person answering, and then repeat back to them the heart of what you heard. This often requires rewording what was said to show your understanding. Having someone to lead this is required. Not recommended to do on your own.

1. What issue would you like to tell me about today?

2. How does this affect your heart and life?

3. If things stay the same, what will that mean for us?

4. What parts of this issue are my responsibility?

5. What parts of this issue are your responsibility?

6. What would you like the future to look like in this area?

7. What could we ask God for in this area?

8. After all we've talked about, what one thing has to change?

9. What are some practical things we can do to make that happen?

After each question is answered, the person asking the questions responds with, "What I hear you saying is…" and then repeats back the heart of what was said. The person answering the questions can respond whether they got it right or if there is more to say. Continue this process until the person answering feels their heart was heard.

Once you have moved through all the questions, change roles. The question-asker now gets to answer and the answer-giver gets to ask questions. Write down the practical things that are decided in question 10, so both people can refer back to what they decided.

VOWS AND JUDGMENTS

Definition of judgment: forming an opinion or evaluation by discerning and comparing, forming an opinion or estimate.

Definition of vow: a solemn promise, one by which a person is bound to an act, service, or condition.

Sometimes in response to what we see in other people's lives, we make judgments about their character, their decisions, or their lives. When we make judgments, we often make vows as well. This can look like seeing the flaws in the character of one or both of our parents, and promising ourselves that we will never be like them. (Judgment: my mom can never keep up with keeping the house clean. Vow: when I grow up, I will always keep my house clean. Or, judgment: my dad has anger issues and I do not want to forgive him. Vow: I will never be like my Dad.) The problem with these promises we make to ourselves, is what we have judged actually can create the exact same fruit in our lives. Making a judgment brings a legal right for the enemy to bring the same pattern in our lives.

Matt 7:1-5 says, Judge not, that you be not judged. For with what judgment you judge, you will be judged; and with the measure you use, it will be measured back to you. And why do you look at the speck in your brother's eye, but do not consider the plank in your own eye? Or how can you say to your brother, 'Let me remove the speck from your eye'; and look, a plank is in your own eye? Hypocrite! First remove the plank from your own eye, and then you will see clearly to remove the speck from your brother's eye.

In order to break the legal right of judgments or vows we have made, we need to repent, renounce, and break agreement with the vow or judgment. This does not mean that someone's behavior was okay, or that we want to be like them, but it does mean that we are releasing them to Jesus, for <u>Him</u> to be the judge of their heart, not us. Sometimes people use vows as a way to cope with life circumstances that are very difficult, but creating a list of rules for yourself to follow, puts your life in a box. If you break any of your own rules, you will be angry with yourself. Often, vows also go along with perfectionism and being hard on yourself. Sometimes we need to forgive ourselves for not being perfect, in order to move away from the habit of making vows we can't keep. Only by being changed from the inside out, having Jesus heal our hearts, can true change happen in our lives.

Use Vows and Judgements Prayer for ministry.

TRAINING

Manifestations

A demonic manifestation is a visible or physical reaction to the anointing, often during prayer or deliverance. In Luke 9:39, a boy possessed by a spirit is described as suddenly screaming, convulsing, and foaming at the mouth—clear biblical evidence that demons can react violently when confronted. The most common manifestations include burping, yawning, crying, coughing, shaking, or vomiting. These are often signs that a demon is being stirred or is about to leave. It's important to distinguish this from what occurs when a **"part"** surfaces in someone with **Dissociative Identity Disorder (DID).** (See the section on DID for more information.) Parts may also speak or respond emotionally, but they are part of the person and should be treated with compassion and care. We do not have conversations with demons, it can lead us down a "bunny trail," but we minister to parts with the love and truth of Jesus, always led by the Holy Spirit.

Cautions in Deliverance

Deliverance is not a formula—it's a Spirit-led process of partnering with Jesus to bring freedom. While this manual provides tools and structure, it is vital to remember: **no two sessions are alike.** God moves differently with each person. We do not minister mechanically; we listen and respond to the Holy Spirit at every step. Our job is not to drive a process, but to yield to what the Lord is doing in that moment. Deliverance is holy work— **we GET to set people free**—and it must be done with humility, compassion, and reverence.

Teamwork and safety are essential. Jesus sent His disciples out two by two (Luke 10:1), and we follow that model. **Never minister deliverance alone.** This protects everyone involved—spiritually, emotionally, and legally. Always have a **signed consent form** before beginning a session, and we strongly recommend having the **completed questionnaire** ahead of time. These tools not only protect you, but also help identify patterns, entry points, and areas the Lord may want to address.

When working in teams, lean into one another's gifts – every member is needed. **Honor the Holy Spirit, but honor one another too.** Always ask before laying hands on someone; trauma survivors may not feel safe with physical touch. If you need to lay hands on someone of the opposite gender, ask a team member of the same gender to place their hand first, then you may place your hand on top—or use a Bible as a point of contact.

We also advise operating under **apostolic or pastoral covering.** Deliverance ministry should never exist in isolation. Accountability, prayer support, and oversight are part of staying spiritually healthy and protected. Most importantly, never become fixated on demons.

Deliverance isn't about showcasing the power of darkness—it's about **revealing the power and love of Jesus Christ.** The goal is always **transformation**—a life made whole, walking in freedom, truth, and identity in Christ. Maintain a **safe, Spirit-filled environment** where clients can encounter God's presence and leave changed.

The Authority of the Believer

Every born-again believer in Jesus Christ has been given authority to cast out demons and walk in victory over the power of the enemy. This authority does **not** come from our own strength, experience, or gifting—it comes from the finished work of **Jesus Christ.** Because we are seated with Him in heavenly places and filled with His Spirit, we have been authorized to continue His works on the earth.

Jesus Himself modeled deliverance throughout the Gospels and then **commissioned His followers** to do the same. This means you don't have to be a pastor or leader to minister deliverance—you just need to understand your identity and stand in your God-given authority.

Below are foundational Scriptures that establish and explain the believer's authority over darkness:

- **Mark 16:17**

  "And these signs will follow those who believe: In My name they will cast out demons..."

- **Luke 10:19**

  "Behold, I give you the authority to trample on serpents and scorpions, and over all the power of the enemy, and nothing shall by any means hurt you."

- **John 14:12**

  "Truly, truly, I say to you, whoever believes in Me will also do the works that I do; and greater works than these will he do, because I am going to the Father."

- **Ephesians 1:22**

  "And He put all things under His feet and gave Him as head over all things to the church"

- **Ephesians 2:6**

  "And God raised us up with Christ and seated us with Him in the heavenly realms in Christ Jesus..."

- **Matthew 10:1**

  "And He called to Him His twelve disciples and gave them authority over unclean spirits, to cast

them out, and to heal every disease and every affliction."

- **Acts 1:8**
  "But you will receive power when the Holy Spirit has come upon you, and you will be My witnesses"

- **1 John 4:4**
  "He who is in you is greater than he who is in the world."

- **2 Corinthians 10:3–4**
  "For though we walk in the flesh, we are not waging war according to the flesh. For the weapons of our warfare are not of the flesh but have divine power to destroy strongholds."

- **James 4:7**
  "Submit yourselves therefore to God. Resist the devil, and he will flee from you."

Reminder: Authority in deliverance doesn't come from using the right formula, doing everything perfectly, or being loud or dramatic. It's not our system or performance that breaks strongholds—it's the anointing that breaks the yoke *(Isaiah 10:27)*. We walk in true authority as we realize who we are in Christ—sons and daughters filled with the Spirit of God. It is His power flowing through us that causes every other name, spirit, and stronghold to bow to the Name above every name: Jesus Christ. When we stay submitted to Him, full of the Word and led by the Holy Spirit, the enemy cannot stand against us.

Selecting Team Members

When building a deliverance team, the most important qualification is a heart fully devoted to God. Choose people who put Him first in their lives—who consistently spend time in prayer, worship, and the Word, and who hunger to grow in their relationship with Him. Authority flows from intimacy; it's in the Presence of God that boldness, discernment, and power are cultivated. Look for those who know how—or are actively learning how—to enter into His Presence. As you form your team, take time to discern each person's spiritual gifts and identify the areas they're passionate to grow in. Placing people where they'll thrive not only helps them develop but also strengthens the team. A healthy deliverance team flows together, with each member contributing their unique anointing under the leadership of the Holy Spirit.

Understanding DID (Dissociative Identity Disorder)

Dissociative Identity Disorder (DID), formerly known as Multiple Personality Disorder (MPD), develops in response to extreme trauma, often beginning in early childhood. During inner healing or deliverance sessions, **"parts"** of a person's heart may come forward. These parts are not demons—they are **fragments of the soul** that may carry pain, memories, emotions, demons, and/or programming. In satanic ritual abuse (SRA), this splitting is done intentionally to create parts for control and manipulation of the individual. However, in trauma-based DID, the splitting is the soul's attempt to survive **overwhelming conflict, pain, fear, or shame**. God actually created our brains with this ability, so that we can continue to function even if those around us make decisions that cause deep pain in our lives. Once this way to keep functioning is no longer needed, Jesus can heal and restore a person's heart! "He heals the broken hearted and binds up their wounds"! (Ps. 147:3)

Many parts are **age-arrested**, meaning they remain emotionally and mentally stuck at the age the trauma occurred. These parts may present as children—frightened, confused, or angry—and they need gentle ministry led by the Holy Spirit.

DID exists on a spectrum. On the **less severe end**, individuals may have "fractures"— not fully developed identities, but pockets of pain or emotion that need the healing presence of Jesus. On the **more severe end**, a person may have multiple distinct parts that can "switch," showing changes in voice, posture, memory, or personality. It's essential to understand: **you can cast out demons, but you cannot cast out a part of someone's heart.** Parts need love, truth, and the gentle healing of Jesus. Deliverance and inner healing work together, but discernment is crucial.

It is important to note that **we do not diagnose clients with DID.** Telling someone they have DID or are a survivor of SRA can be very frightening and confusing for someone not ready to accept that. Often ministry can be done without having to explain, and Jesus can heal even before someone realizes what they needed! Allow Holy Spirit to reveal to the client what he or she needs to know about their trauma, and do not push them into things they are not ready to hear. This way you may be able to avoid having some clients "spiral" and struggle emotionally. As they learn who they are in Christ, they will often become more able to see trauma for what it is, and receive deeper understanding!

For those interested in further training in DID-specific healing, here are some ministries that specialize in this area:

- RGM Connect-https://www.rgmconnect.com/
- Restoration in Christ Ministries (RCM)-https://rcm-usa.org/
- Bride Ministries-https://bridemovement.com/

Further Training: If you are interested in further training on any of these tools, or would like to schedule a school to train and equip your team, reach out to us at teiamartinezministries.com, 719-398-1825

PART FOUR:

RESOURCES

ADULT MINISTRY QUESTIONNAIRE

Confidential Information Cover Sheet

It is the desire of this ministry staff to help you and effectively move you onward in your walk with God.

We believe that through the power of God's Holy Spirit and by His Word, people are changed and transformed into the likeness of Jesus Christ, making us able and capable vessels to advance the Kingdom of God around the world.

We also recognize that we have carried with us baggage from our varied experiences and backgrounds that hinder our spiritual growth and capacity to become fully capable to love and serve Him as He desires. Therefore, it is our goal to minister to you by coming alongside you and assisting you in dealing with the things that hinder your Christian growth and maturity.

To start this process, we are asking you to complete the enclosed questionnaire and return it to us. Please prayerfully consider your response to each question, asking the Holy Spirit to enlighten you.

You can email this form back to us at office@teiamartinezministries.com, or bring it in at your initial appointment.

All information is strictly confidential.

We are a faith-based ministry and therefore we ask that you give a tax-deductible donation for the ministry you receive.

Teia Martinez

(719)398-1825

- CONFIDENTIAL INFORMATION -

Name:_____ Today's Date:_____

Address: _____ Spiritual Counselor:_____

Church Attended: _____

Email:_____ Pastor's Name:_____

Phone: _____ Cell:_____

Age:_____ Birthday: _____ Gender:_____

1. Marital Status: Single   Married   Divorced   Remarried   Widowed

2. Would you say you have a good relationship with your Husband or Wife? Yes
   No

Please explain

3. Children?   Yes No   How many_____

4. Miscarriages?   How many_____

5. Abortions?   How many_____

6. What is your church background? Denomination(s) and/or church experience?

7. When did you accept Jesus Christ into your life? _____

8. Briefly describe your conversion experience:

9. Was your life really changed?   Yes   No
   If so, how?

10. Have you been baptized in water since your conversion?   Yes   No
    If yes, when_____

11. Do you have assurance of your salvation?   Yes   No
    If no, please explain:

12. Have you been filled with the Holy Spirit?   Yes   No
    If yes, when _____ and what is the evidence, you have seen?

13. Describe the content and frequency of your personal devotion and prayer time:

14. Where were you born? (city, state, nation)

_____,_____,_____

15. Have you lived in other countries?   Yes   No
If yes, which ones?

16. Have you traveled to other countries?   Yes   No
If yes, which ones?

Family Background **and Relationships**   (circle all answers that apply)

17. Where was your father born? (City, State, Nation)_____
18. Where was your mother born? (City, State, Nation)_____

19.	Were you a planned child?	Yes	No	Don't know
20.	Were you the "right sex?"	Yes	No	Don't know
21.	Were you conceived out of wedlock?	Yes	No	Don't know
22.	Were you adopted?	Yes	No	Don't know

If yes, at what age? _____
If yes, do you know your natural parents?   Yes   No

23. Was your mother in trauma during pregnancy with you? Yes No Don't know
If yes, please explain:

24. Were you "bonded" at birth?   Yes No Don't know

25. Are your parents living?   Father   Yes No Don't know
                             Mother Yes No Don't know
If no, how old were you when they died? Father_____ Mother_____

26. Are your parents Christians?   Father   Yes No Don't know
                            Mother Yes No Don't know

27. In whose home(s) were you raised?
___Both biological parent's home   ___Adoptive parent's   ___Mother's home
___Father's home   ___Grandparent's home   ___Orphanage
___Foster home(s)   ___Friend's home   ___Other relative's home

28. Were you raised in a Christian home?   Yes No

29. Was (is) your father: Passive Strong and manipulative   Neither
Would you say you had a good relationship with your father? Yes No
Would your father say you had a good relationship with him? Yes No Don't know
Briefly describe your past and present relationship with your father:

30. Was (is) your mother: Passive Strong and manipulative   Neither
Would you say you had a good relationship with your mother? Yes No

Would your mother say you had a good relationship with her? Yes No Don't know
Briefly describe your past and present relationship with your mother:

31. Was your upbringing in an alcoholic or drug dominated home? Yes No
If yes, please briefly explain:

32. Do you have brothers or sisters?   Yes No

Names: 1. _____ Age _____ brother / sister / full / half / step
2. _____ Age _____ brother / sister / full / half / step
3. _____ Age _____ brother / sister / full / half / step
4. _____ Age _____ brother / sister / full / half / step
5. _____ Age _____ brother / sister / full / half / step
6. _____ Age _____ brother / sister / full / half / step

(circle all that apply)

33. Where do you fall in the sibling line? _____
34. Briefly describe your relationship with your siblings while you were growing up:
35. Briefly describe your relationship with your siblings today:
36. Was yours a happy home during childhood?   Yes   No
37. Were you lonely as a teenager?   Yes   No
    Briefly explain:
38. How would you describe your family's financial situation when you were a child?
    _____ Poor   _____ Below Average   _____ Average   _____ Above average   _____ Highly Affluent
39. Do you tithe?   Yes   No

40. Was (is) your father a perfectionist?   Yes   No
41. Was (is) your mother a perfectionist?   Yes   No
42. Were you raised in a physically or verbally abusive home?   Yes   No
    If yes, please briefly explain

43. Were you sexually abused at home?   Yes   No
    If yes, please briefly explain:

44. Were you ever sexually abused outside the home?   Yes   No
    If yes, please briefly explain:

45. Have you, your spouse, your parents or grandparents been in any of the following cults:

___ Occultism   ___ Rosicrucian   ___ Jehovah's Witnesses
___ Gurus   ___ Unity   ___ Spiritist churches
___ Children of Love   ___ Christadelphians   ___ Scientology
___ Bahai   ___ Religious communes   ___ Theosophy
___ Native religions   ___ Unification church   ___ Islam
___ Hinduism   ___ Buddhism   ___ Christian Science
___ Mormons
Others:_____

If you have checked any of the above, state who, what, when and to what extent:

46. Have you, your spouse, your parents or grandparents been a member of any of the following:

___ Freemasons (Masonic Lodges)   ___ Oddfellows   ___ Rainbow Girls
___ Ku Klux Klan   ___ Eastern Star   ___ Shriners
___ Elks club   ___ DeMolay

___ Job's Daughters   ___ Daughter of the Nile
___ Others_____

If you have checked any of the above, state who, what, when and to what extent:

47.   Have you, your spouse, your parents, or grandparents suffered from any of the following:

___High Fever   ___Arthritis   ___Cancer   ___Virus Infections
___Asthma   ___Hay fever   ___Allergies   ___Impotency
___Bent body   ___ Multiple sclerosis ___Muscular Dystrophy ___Diabetes
___Blindness   ___Blood disease   ___Lingering Disorders
___Mental Problems   ___Alcoholism   ___Drug use___RX Tranquilizers
Others_____

If you have checked any of the above, state who, what, when and to what extent:

48.   Did either of your parents suffer from depression?   Father   Mother
       Neither

If you circled mother or father, describe their depression and its impact at home:

This is about you:

49.   Are you easily frustrated?   Yes   No
       If yes, do you show it or bury it?   Show   Bury
       If yes, state what frustrates you:

50.   Would you describe yourself as:
Anxious   Yes   No
A worrier   Yes   No
Depressed   Yes   No

51.   Have you personally ever had psychiatric counseling? Yes   No   When?
_____

52.   Have you ever been hypnotized?   Yes   No

53.   Do you feel mentally confused?   Yes   No

54.   Do you daydream or have mental fantasies?   Yes   No
55.   Do you suffer from frequent bad dreams/nightmare?   Yes   No
       Describe any recurring theme:

56.   Have you ever been attempted to commit suicide?   Yes   No
       If yes, when and why?

57.   Have you tried to commit suicide?   Yes   No
       If yes, how, when and why?

58.   Have you ever wished to die?   Yes   No

59.   Have you been involved in occultism or witchcraft?   Yes   No
60.   Have you ever had involvement with any of the following:

___Fortune Tellers   ___Tarot Cards   ___Ouija boards   ___Séances
___Mediums   ___Palmistry   ___Astrology   ___Color Therapy
___Levitation   ___Astral Travel   ___Horoscopes   ___Lucky Charms
___Black Magic   ___White Magic   ___Demon Worship   ___Spirit Guides
___Clairvoyance   ___Crystals   ___Automatic Handwriting___Native Healer
___Dungeons & Dragons ___New Age Movement   ___Witch Doctors   ___Voodoo
Others_____

Describe your involvement with any of the above:

61. Have you ever read books on occultism or witchcraft? Yes No
  If yes, what and why?

62. Have you made any pacts with Satan? Yes No
63. Do you know of any curse placed on you or your family? Yes No
  If yes, when, by whom and why?

64. Have you been involved in transcendental meditation? Yes No
65. Have you been involved in Eastern religions? Yes No
66. Have you ever visited heathen/pagan temples? Yes No
67. Have you ever done any form of Yoga? Yes No
68. Have you learned/used mind communication or mind control? Yes No
69. Have you been involved in Splankna? Yes No
  If yes, when, by whom and why?

70. Have you ever seen a demonic presence? Yes No

71. Do you currently have in your home any symbols of idols or spirit worship such as:

____Buddha	____Totem Poles	____Painted Facemasks
____Idol Carvings	____Fetish Objects or Feather	____Pagan Symbols
____Tikis	____Native Art	____Kachina Dolls
____Crystals	____Healing rocks	

72. What type of music did you occupy your mind with before conversion?

____Rock & Roll	____Punk Rock	____New Age
____Rap/Hip Hop	____Heavy Metal	____Country
____Gospel/Christian	____Classical	____Contemporary

73. Have you ever learned any of the martial arts? Yes No
  If yes, describe and explain:

74. Do you have any tattoos? Yes No
How many? _____

75. Have you ever utilized any of the following drugs?

___LSD	___Speed	___Marijuana
___Cocaine	___Crack	___Uppers
___Downers	___Other drugs	

Were you addicted: Yes No

76. Have you been addicted to any of the following:

___Gambling	___Compulsive Exercise	___Being a Spendthrift
___Television	___Alcohol	___Smoking
___Food	___Coffee	___Shopping
___Pornography	___Sex	___RX

Drugs_____

For questions 77 through 92 please CIRCLE "P" for past, a "C" for current or "PC" for both.

77. <u>In your Christian experience do you:</u>

P | C | PC Have trouble accepting the deity of Christ.
P | C | PC Have trouble accepting the teachings of Christ.
P | C | PC Tend to gravitate toward humanistic thinking.
P | C | PC Not believe you have an anointing on your life.
P | C | PC Seem to always be persecuted in your walk with Christ.

P | C | PC Have trouble accepting Christ's atoning sacrifice.
P | C | PC Tend to unknowingly suppress ministries.
P | C | PC Tend to have a lawlessness about you.
P | C | PC Tend to often be in heretical teaching.
P | C | PC Have trouble accepting God's forgiveness.

78. I have in the past or currently struggle with the following:

P | C | PC Lust
P | C | PC My ambitions and achievements
P | C | PC Oppression
P | C | PC Religion

P | C | PC Satanic interest
P | C | PC Fear of death
P | C | PC Spiritual blindness
P | C | PC A bound mind

P | C | PC Various forms of corruption
P | C | PC Bitterness
P | C | PC Control over life
P | C | PC Spiritual deadness

79. I have in the past or currently experience problems in the following areas:

P | C | PC Mental illness
P | C | PC Spiritual deafness or blindness
P | C | PC Foaming at the mouth
P | C | PC Pining away
P | C | PC Prostration
P | C | PC Madness
P | C | PC Senility
P | C | PC Epilepsy
P | C | PC Hallucinations
P | C | PC Eating disorders:
Type(s)_____

P | C | PC Ear problems
P | C | PC Crippled
P | C | PC Alzheimer's
P | C | PC Burned
P | C | PC Suicidal
P | C | PC Insanity
P | C | PC Schizophrenia
P | C | PC Paranoia
P | C | PC Palsy

P | C | PC Near drowning experience
P | C | PC Excessive crying or tearing
P | C | PC Gnashing of teeth
P | C | PC Chemical imbalance
P | C | PC Self-mutilation
P | C | PC Retardation
P | C | PC Seizures
P | C | PC Hear voices
P | C | PC Attention deficit

80. I have in the past or currently experience problems in the following areas:

P | C | PC Death seems to be lurking nearby
P | C | PC Clumsiness
P | C | PC Speeding
P | C | PC Death in marriage

P | C | PC Disease
P | C | PC Fighting
P | C | PC Death to ministry
P | C | PC Accidents

P | C | PC Suicide
P | C | PC Dare devil acts
P | C | PC Death in relationships
P | C | PC Random acts of violence

81. I have in the past or currently experience interest with the following areas:

P | C | PC Divination
P | C | PC Stargazing, zodiac, horoscopes
P | C | PC Acupuncture
P | C | PC Spiritists
P | C | PC Warlock
P | C | PC Wizard
P | C | PC Animal guides
P | C | PC Lust for power or control

P | C | PC False Prophecy
P | C | PC Rebellion
P | C | PC Birth charts
P | C | PC Self-will
P | C | PC Witches
P | C | PC Spirit guides
P | C | PC Astral projection
P | C | PC Ghosts

P | C | PC Fortune telling or soothsayers
P | C | PC Hypnotist-enchanter
P | C | PC Magic (Black or white)
P | C | PC Mind control / manipulation
P | C | PC Sorcerer
P | C | PC Vampires
P | C | PC Water witching

82. I have in the past or currently struggle with the following areas:

P | C | PC Error in doctrine
P | C | PC Hyper spirituality
P | C | PC Mix the holy with the profane
P | C | PC New Age movement
P | C | PC Maintaining a form of godliness
P | C | PC Dullness of comprehension
P | C | PC Hindrances to hearing sermons
P | C | PC Hindrances to believing faith principals.
P | C | PC False doctrines such as Mormonism, Catholicism, Buddhism, Hinduism, Unitarianism

P | C | PC False prophecy
P | C | PC Twisting of scripture
P | C | PC Defensive
P | C | PC Contentiousness
P | C | PC Mental confusion
P | C | PC Hindrances to prayer
P | C | PC Hindrances to movement of the Holy Spirit

P | C | PC An un-submissive attitude
P | C | PC Unteachable spirit
P | C | PC Argumentative
P | C | PC Servant to corruption
P | C | PC Fears
P | C | PC Hindrances to Bible study

83. I am or have in the past been involved in the following areas:

P | C | PC Familiar Spirits
P | C | PC Calling on Mediums
P | C | PC Inferiority
P | C | PC False prophecy
P | C | PC Racism
P | C | PC Self pity

P | C | PC Divination
P | C | PC Yoga
P | C | PC Mind dreaming
P | C | PC Séances
P | C | PC Low self esteem
P | C | PC Necromancing

P | C | PC Witchcraft
P | C | PC Clairvoyant
P | C | PC Spirit guides / animal guides
P | C | PC Bigotry
P | C | PC Peeping and muttering
P | C | PC Drugs, illegal or prolonged use of legal

84. I have in the past or currently struggle with the following:

P | C | PC Fear
P | C | PC Introvert
P | C | PC Anxiety, stress
P | C | PC Lack of trust, doubt, worry
P | C | PC Fear of abandonment
P | C | PC Fear of failure
P | C | PC A critical spirit
P | C | PC Fear of not being good enough
P | C | PC Other fears, list_____

P | C | PC Torment – horror
P | C | PC A desire to be a hermit or recluse
P | C | PC Extrovert
P | C | PC Migraines
P | C | PC Fear of heart attacks
P | C | PC Fear of heights
P | C | PC Panic attacks
P | C | PC Fear of animals

P | C | PC Fear of death
P | C | PC Fear of saying 'no'
P | C | PC Fear of rejection
P | C | PC Fear of authority
P | C | PC A constant desire to be alone
P | C | PC Fear of spiders
P | C | PC Unhealthy fear of God

85. I have in the past or currently struggle with the following:

P | C | PC Haughtiness
P | C | PC Scornful attitude
P | C | PC Regional pride
P | C | PC Self-righteous
P | C | PC Overbearing or domineering
P | C | PC Rejection of man's authority
P | C | PC Exalted feelings
P | C | PC Self-deception
P | C | PC Strife
P | C | PC Attention seeking
P | C | PC Always right type of attitude

P | C | PC With religious pride
P | C | PC Vanity
P | C | PC Obstinate
P | C | PC Dictatorial
P | C | PC Manipulative
P | C | PC Rebellion
P | C | PC Gossip
P | C | PC Contentiousness
P | C | PC Idleness
P | C | PC Interrupting others
P | C | PC Being arrogant and smug

P | C | PC Rationalizing pride
P | C | PC Professional pride
P | C | PC National pride
P | C | PC Controlling
P | C | PC Rejection of God's authority
P | C | PC A 'holier-than-thou' attitude
P | C | PC Egotistical attitude
P | C | PC Bragging and boastful attitude
P | C | PC Performance orientation
P | C | PC Impatience

86. I have in the past or currently struggle with the following areas:

P | C | PC Self-hate
P | C | PC Many regrets
P | C | PC Depression
P | C | PC Gluttony
P | C | PC Continuous sorrow and grief
P | C | PC Hopelessness
P | C | PC Abandonment
P | C | PC Suppressed emotions

P | C | PC Self-pity
P | C | PC Life's unfairness
P | C | PC Excessive mourning
P | C | PC Loneliness
P | C | PC Discouragement
P | C | PC Rejection
P | C | PC Inferiority
P | C | PC Insomnia

P | C | PC A broken heart
P | C | PC Suicidal thoughts
P | C | PC Inner hurts and a torn spirit
P | C | PC Dejection
P | C | PC Despair
P | C | PC Insecurity
P | C | PC Low self-esteem
P | C | PC False responsibility

87. I have in the past or currently suffer from the following infirmities:

P | C | PC Infirmity in general
P | C | PC Extended fever
P | C | PC Lameness
P | C | PC Oppression
P | C | PC Tumors
P | C | PC Cysts
P | C | PC Viral infections
P | C | PC Hay fever
P | C | PC Seizures
P | C | PC Covid-19

P | C | PC Bent body-spine
P | C | PC Impotency
P | C | PC Arthritis
P | C | PC Tuberculosis
P | C | PC Lingering disorders
P | C | PC Warts
P | C | PC Bacterial infections
P | C | PC Allergies
P | C | PC Leukemia
P | C | PC Covid vaccine

P | C | PC Chemical imbalance
P | C | PC Frailness
P | C | PC Diabetes
P | C | PC Emphysema
P | C | PC Excessive pain and affliction
P | C | PC Excessive fatigue
P | C | PC Asthma
P | C | PC Epilepsy
P | C | PC Hypochondria
P | C | PC Cancer: List type(s)_____

88. I have in the past or currently struggle with the following:

P | C | PC Jealousy
P | C | PC Cruelty
P | C | PC Coveting
P | C | PC Strife
P | C | PC Anger and rage
P | C | PC Suppressed anger

P | C | PC Revenge
P | C | PC Extreme competition
P | C | PC Selfishness
P | C | PC Contentiousness
P | C | PC Violence
P | C | PC Suppressed rage

P | C | PC Spite
P | C | PC Causing divisions
P | C | PC Envy
P | C | PC Hatred
P | C | PC Bigotry and racism
P | C | PC Desire to murder

89. I have in the past or continue to struggle with the following:

P | C | PC Lying
P | C | PC Strong deception
P | C | PC Exaggeration
P | C | PC Accusations
P | C | PC Superstitions
P | C | PC Shame
P | C | PC Self-deception

P | C | PC Flattery
P | C | PC False prophecy
P | C | PC False teaching
P | C | PC Religious bondage
P | C | PC Profanity
P | C | PC Condemnation
P | C | PC False burdens

P | C | PC Driving zeal
P | C | PC Gossip
P | C | PC Slander
P | C | PC Covenant breaking
P | C | PC Guilt
P | C | PC Melancholy nature
P | C | PC Frenzied emotional actions

90. I have in the past or continue to struggle with the following:

P | C | PC Perversity
P | C | PC Past abortion
P | C | PC Masturbation
P | C | PC Sexual perversions
P | C | PC Molestation
P | C | PC Date rape
P | C | PC Computer pornography
P | C | PC Contentious
P | C | PC Homosexuality
P | C | PC Rebellion
P | C | PC Effeminate Spirit

P | C | PC Broken spirit
P | C | PC Child abuse
P | C | PC Atheism
P | C | PC Doctrinal error
P | C | PC Incest
P | C | PC Spousal rape
P | C | PC Chronic worrier
P | C | PC Foolishness
P | C | PC Lesbianism
P | C | PC Sexual frigidity
P | C | PC Fornication

P | C | PC Evil actions
P | C | PC Prostitution
P | C | PC A filthy mind
P | C | PC Twisting the word
P | C | PC Rape
P | C | PC Pornography
P | C | PC Self lover
P | C | PC Lust
P | C | PC Vain imaginations
P | C | PC Emotional frigidity
P | C | PC Adultery

91. I have in the past or continue to struggle with the following:

P | C | PC Seducing spirits
P | C | PC Fascination with evil ways
P | C | PC Fascination with evil objects
P | C | PC Fascination with evil people
P | C | PC Attracted to false wonders

P | C | PC Seared conscience
P | C | PC Seducers
P | C | PC Wander from the truth
P | C | PC Attracted to false signs
P | C | PC Jezebel Spirit

P | C | PC Deception
P | C | PC Enticers
P | C | PC Hypocritical lies
P | C | PC Attracted to false prophets
P | C | PC Ahab spirit (passivity)

92. I have in the past or continue to struggle with the following:

P | C | PC Addiction to entertainment
P | C | PC Prostitution of Spirit, Soul or Body
P | C | PC Worldliness
P | C | PC Chronic dissatisfaction
P | C | PC Addiction to sports

P | C | PC Unfaithfulness
P | C | PC Love of money
P | C | PC Fornication
P | C | PC Love of self
P | C | PC Addiction to television

P | C | PC Adultery
P | C | PC Excessive appetite
P | C | PC Idolatry
P | C | PC Self reward

93. Please describe as clearly as you can what is going on in your life at this time. What was it that prompted you to seek spiritual counseling?

_____
_____
_____
_____
_____

What do I think?

Please place a check by each statement that describes your thinking about yourself!

94.

___I am all alone.
___I don't matter.
___God has forsaken me, too.
___I cannot trust anyone.

___I have been overlooked.
___No one ever really cares.
___There is no one to protect me.
___I am afraid they won't come back.

___They do not need me.
___They are not coming back.
___No one will believe me.
___I cannot trust pastors/ministers.

95.

___I am so stupid, ignorant, an idiot.
___I was a participant.
___I should have done something to have stopped it from happening.
___I knew what was going to happen, yet I stayed away.
___I felt pleasure so I must have wanted it.
___It happened because of my looks, my gender, my body, etc.
___I did not try to run away.
___I was paid for services rendered.
___I kept going back.
___I'm bad, dirty, shameful, sick, nasty.

___I allowed it.
___I should have known better.
___It was all my fault.
___I should have told someone.
___I was a participant.
___I should have stopped them.
___I am cheap like a slut.
___I deserved it.
___I did it to him/her first.
___I am just in the way.

96.

___I am going to die.
___I do not know what to do.
___If I trust I will die.
___It is just a matter of time before it happens again.
___If I let him/her/them into my life they will hurt me, too.
___Something bad will happen if I tell, stop it, confront it.

___He/she is going to hurt me.
___If I tell, they will come back and hurt me.
___He/she/they are coming back.
___They are going to get me.
___Doom is just around the corner.

97.

___He/she/they are too strong to resist.
___I am going to die and I cannot do anything about it.
___I am too weak to resist.
___I cannot get away.
___I am overwhelmed.
___Everything is out of control.
___Not even God can help me.

___I cannot stop this.
___There is no way out.
___The pain is too great to bear.
___I cannot get loose.
___I don't know what to do.
___I am pulled from every direction.
___I am too small to do anything.

98.

___I am dirty, evil, shameful, perverted, because of what happened to me.
___No one will be able to really love me.
___Everyone can see my shame, filth, dirtiness, etc.
___I will always be hurt/damaged/broken because of what has happened.
___God could never want me after what has happened to me.

___My life is ruined.
___I will never be happy.
___I will always be unclean, filthy, etc.
___My body parts are dirty.
___I will never feel clean again.

99.

___I am not loved, needed, cared for, or important.
___I am worthless and have no value.
___I was a mistake.
___I was never liked by them, because I was _____!
___I am in the way; I am a burden.
she.
___I could never jump high enough to please him/her.

___They do not need me.
___I am unimportant.
___I should have never been born.
___God could never love or accept me.
___I could never be as_____as he or

___I am not acceptable.

100.

___It is never going to get any better.
___It will just happen again and again.
___I have no reason to live.
___I just want to die.

___There is no way out.
___There is no good thing for me.
___There are no options for me.
___Nothing good will ever come of this.

101.

___I don't know what is happening to me.
___This does not make any sense.

___Everything is confusing.
___Why would they do this to me?

Other Areas of Your Life

102.   Do you have known sin, unforgiveness, resentment, bitterness or hatred toward anyone? (List all and use the back of this page if needed.) Whom and why:

_____

_____

_____

_____

_____

103.   Have you completed Cleansing Stream?   Yes   No

If yes, state where? _____. The month and year of the retreat: Month_____ Year_____
Please describe your experience:

_____

_____

_____

_____

_____

104.   Besides Cleansing Stream, have you received prayer for deliverance?   Yes   No
If yes, describe your experience:

_____

_____

_____

_____

_____

_____

105.   Describe your dreams, your goals and aspirations for your life?

_____

_____

_____

_____

_____

106.   Are there any other problems you believe this questionnaire has not addressed? Please explain:

_____

_____

_____

_____

_____

_____

"The Spirit of the Sovereign Lord is on me, because the Lord has anointed me to preach good news to the poor. He has sent me to bind up the brokenhearted, to proclaim freedom for the captives and release for the prisoners, to proclaim the year of the Lord's favor."

Isaiah 61:1-2

TEEN MINISTRY QUESTIONNAIRE

Confidential Cover Sheet: Teens

It is our desire to see your children and family healed and empowered to live and enjoy the abundant life that Jesus desires us to have.

I believe it is God's will for us to be healed and empowered, to build families to impact the world for Jesus. We have recognized that there is an adversary in this world that stands against our children and families to prevent us from being mighty vessels of God.

In order to help you, please complete the enclosed questionnaires for you and your teen. It is very important that the parent(s) completes the adult questionnaire(s) also as it will bring helpful insight to your child's healing. Please have the teenager complete Section One and parent(s) complete Section Two.

We have attached both the teen and adult questionnaires. You can send this form back by e-mail to office@teiamartinezministries.com or bring to your first appointment.

All information is strictly confidential.

TEEN MINISTRY QUESTIONNAIRE AGES 13-17 YEARS

(To be completed by teen if able, if not able parent please complete)

Date _____

Parent's Name_____

Parent/Emergency Cell Phone _____

Parent's Email_____

Teen's Name_____

Teen's Cell (optional) _____

Address_____

Age_____ DOB_____ Gender M   F

Section One: Questions For Teen

1. How was your relationship with your mother as a child?

2. How is your relationship with your mother as a teenager?

3. How was your relationship with your dad as a child?

4. How is your relationship with your dad as a teenager?

5. How were your relationships with your siblings as a child?

6. How are your relationships with your siblings as a teenager?

7. Were you adopted?   Yes   No

8. Were you a planned child? Yes   No   Don't Know

9. Were you the "right" sex? Yes   No   Don't Know

10. Did your mother suffer from trauma during your pregnancy? Yes No Don't Know

11. Did you have a complicated birth? Yes   No   Don't Know

12. Where do you fall in the sibling birth order?

13. How many siblings do you have? Name & ages

14. Habits: Bite nails   Suck Thumb   Wet the bedPull/twist your hair
    Other habits/behaviors: _____

15. Do you strive to please people?

16. Do you judge others?

17. Do you find you act your age most of the time or are people telling you to grow up?

18. What do I feel?

Please place a check by each statement that sometimes feels true, even if you know it is not true!

___I am all alone.   ___I have been overlooked.   ___They do not need me.

___I don't matter.   ___No one ever really cares.   ___They are not coming back

___God has forsaken me, too.   ___There is no one to protect me.   ___No one will believe me.

___I cannot trust anyone.   ___I am afraid they won't come back   ___I cannot trust pastors/ministers.

___I am so stupid, ignorant, an idiot.   ___I allowed it.

___I was a participant.   ___I should have known better.

___I should have done something to have stopped it from happening.   ___It was all my fault.

___I knew what was going to happen, yet I stayed away.   ___I should have told someone.

___I felt pleasure so I must have wanted it.   ___I was a participant.

___It happened because of my looks, my gender, my body, etc.   ___I should have stopped them.

___I did not try to run away.   ___I am cheap like a slut.

___I was paid for services rendered.   ___I deserved it.

___I kept going back.   ___I did it to him/her first.

___I'm bad, dirty, shameful, sick, nasty.   ___I am just in the way.

___I am going to die.   ___He/she is going to hurt me.

____I do not know what to do.   ____If I tell they will come back and hurt me.

____If I trust I will die.   ____He/she/they are coming back.

____It is just a matter of time before it happens again.   ____They are going to get me.

____If I let him/her/them into my life they will hurt me, too

                                  ____Doom is just around the corner.

____Something bad will happen if I tell, stop it, confront it.

____He/she/they are too strong to resist.   ____I cannot stop this.

____I am going to die and I cannot do anything about it.   ____There is no way out.

____I am too weak to resist.   ____The pain is too great to bear.

____I cannot get away.   ____I cannot get loose.

____I am overwhelmed.   ____I don't know what to do.

____Everything is out of control.   ____I am pulled from every direction.

____Not even God can help me.   ____I am too small to do anything.

                                  ____My life is ruined.

____I am dirty, evil, shameful, perverted, because of what happened to me.

____No one will be able to really love me.   ____I will never be happy.

____Everyone can see my shame, filth, dirtiness, etc.   ____I will always be unclean, filthy

____I will always be hurt/damaged/broken because of what has happened.

                                  ____My body parts are dirty.

____God could never want me after what has happened to me.

                                  ____I will never feel clean again.

___I am not loved, needed, cared for, or important.   ___They do not need me.

___I am worthless and have no value.   ___I am unimportant.

___I was a mistake.   ___I should have never been born.

___I was never liked by them, because I was _____!

___God could never love or accept me.

___I am in the way; I am a burden.

___I could never be as_____as he or she.

___I could never jump high enough to please him/her.   ___I am not acceptable.

___It is never going to get any better.   ___There is no way out.

___It will just happen again and again.   ___There is no good thing for me.

___I have no reason to live.   ___There are no options for me.

___I just want to die.   ___Nothing good will ever come of this.

___I don't know what is happening to me.   ___Everything is confusing.

___This does not make any sense.   ___Why would they do this to me?

19. Who disciplines in the household?

20. Who makes the rules in the house?

21. Do you feel like your family is: Poor   Rich   Middle class

22. Do you lie or steal?

23. Are you unhappy as a teenager?

24. Are you introvert or extrovert?

25. Have you been bullied? Where has this happened?

26. Have you ever been suicidal?

27. Do you have a hard time forgiving yourself when you do something wrong?

28. Are you a perfectionist?

29. Do you have a hard time receiving love?

30. Is it hard for you to say how you feel?

31. Are either of your parents perfectionists or workaholics?

32. Are you impatient, irritable, moody, rebellious, stubborn, angry, violent? (Circle)

33. Do you cuss?

34. Do you have unforgiveness, resentment, bitterness or hate anyone?

35. Are you easily frustrated? Do you show it or bury it?   Show   Bury

36. Do either of your parents deal with depression, have anxiety, are worriers? Who and what?

37. Have any parents, grandparents, brothers or sisters suffered from mental problems?

38. Have you ever seen a psychiatrist?   Yes No

39. Have you ever been hypnotized?   Yes No

40. Do you ever deal with confusion?   Yes No

41. After you have been hurt, do you ever make vows or promises to yourself? Yes No

42. Do you daydream or fantasize?   Yes No

43. Do you suffer from nightmares? Are they reoccurring?

44. Have you ever had thoughts of death?

45. Do you have any phobias?

46. Do you deal with panic attacks?

Witchcraft

47. Have you ever made agreements or pacts with the devil for power?

48. Have you ever made a blood pact with anyone else?

49. Do you know of anyone cursing your family?

50. Have either of your parents or any grandparent ever been involved in idol worship or witchcraft? Who/what?

51. Have you ever been involved in:

Fortune telling	Mediums	Color therapy
Tarot cards Palm reading	Levitation	Ouija boards
Astrology Astral travel/shifting	Seances	Demon worship
Star signs/horoscopes	Luckycharms	Clairvoyance
Crystals	New age	Black magic

52. What kind of video games do you play? What kind of social media do you use?

53. Have you watched demonic movies? Anime? Witchcraft movies? Vampire movies? (circle or give details)

54. Have you ever been involved in Eastern religions?
yoga   transcendental meditation   chakras   reiki acupuncture

55. Have you ever visited any temples?

56. Have you ever used mind control?

57. Have you ever worn lucky charms or signs of the zodiac?

58. Do you have any idols or spirit worship items? Tikis, buddhas, totem poles, etc.

59. What kind of music do you listen to?

60. Have you ever been a part of martial arts?

61. Do you have any tattoos?

Sexual

62. Do you struggle with lust? Yes   No   Opposite sex   Same sex

63. Do you struggle with masturbation and pornography?

64. Have you ever been sexually abused in the home? Out of the home?

65. Do you have a boyfriend/girlfriend? Are you sexually intimate?

66. Do you have sexual dreams?

Addictions

67. What addictions are known to be in your family?

68. Have you ever been addicted to Alcohol   Smoking   Drugs prescription/non presc   Vaping   Gambling Food Binge eating   Compulsive exercise   Internet Social media Phone

Ethnic/cultural

69. Where were you born?

70. Have you lived in other countries?

71. Where were your mother/father born?

Religious

72. What churches have you attended?

73. Tell me in one word, who Jesus Christ is to you?

74. Are you saved? If so, what has changed?

75. If you were to die, do you believe you would go to Heaven?

76. Is there anything that is hard for you to give up since you've been saved?

77. Do you have a hard time trusting God in everyday living?

78. Do you suffer from any sickness, illness, or allergy?

79. Do you have any other problems you feel this questionnaire has not covered?

COUNSELEE PRAYER AND RENUNCIATION: (TO BE REPEATED BEFORE MINISTRY)

I accept Jesus Christ to be my personal Savior. I renounce all oppression of the evil one in my life because of the iniquity, transgression and sin of my parents, ancestors or myself, and claim release and cleansing through the blood of Jesus Christ. I repent from every sinful attitude, action or habit of mine which does not glorify Jesus Christ and ask for forgiveness, release, cleansing and wholeness. Lord I choose to forgive all those who have hurt me and lay down all anger and rebellion. In particular, I choose to forgive _____. (You may include yourself)

I renounce satan and all demonic influences, bondages, dominations, (sickness, infirmities, allergies) in my life. I claim the release and freedom promised by Jesus Christ, so that He may be LORD of my total personality and be glorified in all I say and do. Amen.

SECTION TWO - PARENTS PLEASE COMPLETE THE FOLLOWING:

REJECTION

1. Was your teenager conceived out of marriage? YES/NO

2. Was your teenager adopted? YES/NO

3. Was your teenager a planned child? YES/NO

4. Did you want a boy and have a girl? YES/NO

5. Did you want a girl and have a boy? YES/NO

6. Did you (the mother) have any trauma during your pregnancy? YES/NO (Please circle: Threatened miscarriage, fearful, suicidal, depression, grief)

7. Were there any complications when he/she was born? YES/NO (Please circle: Cesarean section, long labor, induced, instruments used, cord around neck, premature birth, fast, overdue, etc.)

MENTAL AND EMOTIONAL PROBLEMS

8. Are there any mental problems in the family? YES/NO (Nervous breakdown, bi polar, depression, etc.)

9. Has any member of the family including grandparents been involved in a secret society? YES/NO (Ex.: Freemasonry- secret society especially for men.)

10. Did you or your Mother/Grandmother have a miscarriage or abortion before your teenager was born? YES/NO

11. Is there any premature death (died young) in the family? YES/NO

12. Any family deaths and you don't know why they died? YES/NO Suicides? YES/NO

13. Are there major fears in the family? YES/NO Please name the fears_____

14. Do any of the following freak you out?

Failure	unable to cope	inadequacy
Authority figures	the dark	death
Rape	violence	being alone
Satan and evil spirits	the future	men
Women	crowds	the opinion of people
Insanity	public speak	accident
Death/injury to love ones	heights	enclosed spaces
Commitment to marriage	not being married	divorce or marriage break up
Terminal disease	old age	abandonment

Insects	spiders	dogs
Snakes	animals	water
Pain	loud noises	flying

Open spaces(agoraphobia) other?

15. Have you ever had a panic attack? YES/NO

OCCULT & WITCHCRAFT

16. Are you aware of any curses in the family? YES/NO
(Any poverty, things that just seem to plague your family)

17. Has there been any family involvement in occult or witchcraft practice? YES/NO
(This includes going into temples, etc.)

18. Has there been family involvement with the following (circle)

mediums	palmistry	astrology	star signs
color therapy	Levitation	astral travel	horoscope
lucky charms	pendulum diagnosis	black magic	demon worship
clairvoyance crystals	new age		

19. Any family involvement in Yoga, Pilates? YES/NO

20. Any family involvement in Martial Arts? YES/NO

21. Any family involvement in: warning of future occurrences? YES/NO
deja vu?   YES/NO psychic sight? YES/NO

SEXUAL

22. Is there evidence of LUST in your family going back to your grandparents? YES/NO
(e.g., affairs, divorce, pornography, alternate sexual preferences, children born out of marriage, sexual abuse.)

23. Is there fornication - having sex before marriage? YES/NO

24. Is there adultery - having sex with someone who is married to another person? YES/NO

25. Has there been incest?- sexual touching against family members? YES/NO

26. Has there been any rape?   YES/NO

27. Is there homosexuality?   YES/NO

28. Is there lesbianism? YES/NO

29. Is there bisexuality?   YES/NO

30. Is there bestiality? YES/NO

31. Is there pornography addiction in the family line? YES/NO

32. Have there been abortions in the family line? YES/NO

ADDICTIONS

33. Are there any addictions to the following in the family line?

Alcohol	YES/NO
Smoking (nicotine, vaping)	YES/NO
Drugs (illegal or prescription)	YES/NO
Gambling	YES/NO
Food (obesity, anorexia, bulimia, binge eating)	YES/NO
Compulsive Exercise	YES/NO
Overspending	YES/NO
Electronic Games	YES/NO
Facebook, Social Media, Internet	YES/NO
Phones, texting	YES/NO

CULTURAL

34. Where was your Mother and Father born?
Mother _____ Father _____

35. Where were your Grandparents born?
Mother's mother _____ Mother's father _____
Father's mother _____ Father's father_____

RELIGIOUS

36. Has anyone in the family line been involved in a cult? YES/NO
(Jehovah's witness, Mormons, Christian Science, Scientology, religious communities etc)

37. Does your teen have Social Media accounts? Which One(s)?

38. Does teen live with both parents?

39. Was your teen raised around drugs or alcohol?

40. What kind of video/computer games are played by your teen, or others in home?

41. Was there any situation during pregnancy or prior to now that you can think of that would have been stressful or traumatic on you or the family?

42. Did your teen experience trauma at birth?

43. Does your teen have any bad habits?

44. Has your teen been diagnosed by a Dr with having any disorders?

45. Is your teen currently taking any medications, or have any physical problems/illnesses?

Adopted Children Questions:

46. What age was your child adopted?

47. What country is the child from?

48. Was the child in foster care or an orphanage?

49. Was the teen abused physically or sexually in the foster home or orphanage?

50. Were the biological parents addicted to drugs or alcohol?

51. Have you bonded with your child?

52. Is your teen able to express love?

53. What kind of behavior is the teen exhibiting that has caused you to seek ministry?

54. Are there any other issues with your teen that were not covered?

Luke: 18:16

Let the children come to me, and do not hinder them, for the kingdom of God belongs to such as these.

CHILD MINISTRY QUESTIONNAIRE

Confidential Cover Sheet: Children

It is our desire to see your children and family healed and empowered to live and enjoy the abundant life that Jesus desires us to have.

I believe it is God's will for us to be healed and empowered, to build families to impact the world for Jesus. I have recognized that there is an adversary in this world that stands against our children and families to prevent us from being mighty vessels of God.

In order to help you, please complete the enclosed questionnaires for you and your child. It is very important that the parent(s) completes the adult questionnaire(s) as it will bring helpful insight to your child's healing. If the child is 12-17 years of age please have them complete the teen questionnaire. If your child is able to, allow them to complete as much of the children's questionnaire as possible.

I have attached both the child and adult questionnaires. You can drop off the form or send this form back by e-mail to office@teiamartinezministries.com

All information is strictly confidential.

CHILDREN'S MINISTRY QUESTIONNAIRE AGES 2-12 YEARS

(To be completed by child if able, if not able parent please complete)

Date _____

Parent Name_____ Cell Phone _____

Parent Email_____

Child Name_____

Address_____

Age_____ DOB_____ Gender_____

Questions: (For child)

Are you angry or sad at anyone? Who? _____

Do you get mad at yourself? Why? _____

How do you feel at home? _____

How do you feel at school? _____

Do you get mad at your mom? Why? _____

Do you get mad at your dad? Why? _____

Has anyone ever touched you in a bad way?

Who?_____When?_____Where?_____

Have you seen bad things on the computer?

What did you see? _____

Are there things on the computer, cell phone, or TV that make you feel bad that you have seen?

What are they? _____

Do you touch yourself or others? Yourself _____ Others_____

Do you have bad dreams? Yes _____ No _____

What are they about? _____

What kind of things make you scared? _____

When you get angry what do you do? _____

Do you have an imaginary friend? Yes____ No____

What is your imaginary friend's name? _____

Is it hard to obey mom or dad? Yes___ No___

Do you sometimes hear voices telling you not to obey mom or dad? Yes___ No___

Do you tell lies? Yes___ No___

Do you hit or bite when you're mad? Yes___ No___

Can you write down what you would like to get help with, or do better at?

_____

_____

Parents, Please Complete the Following:

Does child have Social Media accounts?

Which One(s): _____

Does child live with both parents?

Explain: _____

Was child raised around drugs or alcohol?

Explain: _____

_____

What kind of video/computer games are played by child or others in home?

_____

Was there any situation during pregnancy or prior to now that you can think of that would have been stressful or traumatic on you or the family?

If so, please explain: _____

_____

Did child experience trauma at birth?

Explain: _____

_____

Does your child have any bad habits?

Explain: _____

_____

Has your child been diagnosed by a doctor with having any disorders?

If so what: _____

_____

Adoption Questions:

At what age was your child adopted? _____

What country is the child from? _____

Was the child in foster care or an orphanage?

Explain: _____

Was the child abused physically or sexually in the foster home or orphanage?

Explain: _____

Were the biological parents addicted to drugs or alcohol?

Explain: _____

Have you bonded with your child?

Explain: _____

Is your child able to express love?

Explain: _____

_____

What kind of behavior is the child exhibiting that has caused you to seek ministry?

Explain: _____

_____

Luke: 18:16

Let the children come to me, and do not hinder them, for the kingdom of God belongs to such as these.

PERSONAL CONSENT TO RECEIVE MINISTRY

Please Note:

We are a faith-based ministry, and do not charge a fee.

However, we do ask that you prayerfully give a tax-deductible donation for the ministry you receive.

I do hereby affirm and state that I,_____, *Please Print Clearly*

Consent for Teia Martinez Ministries, Inc. and Healing Hearts International Ministries (TMM) and all volunteers working with (TMM) to minister to me in the areas of Spiritual Counseling, Personal Ministry and the Ministry of Deliverance.

I understand and acknowledge that all ministers either licensed or lay that are involved in this ministry are not licensed or trained as psychotherapists, mental health professionals, or professional counselors.

All guidance, counsel, and advice that I receive will be solely based on Scriptural principles and Christian biblical standards as spelled out in the Holy Bible, the written Word of God.

I further understand and acknowledge that all ministry done is solely under the direction and control of the Holy Spirit of God, and that no guarantees are made, nor can be made, with regard to my current or future problems.

I state that I have voluntarily sought this ministry for myself and that I hereby release Healing Hearts International Ministries, Inc. (TMM) and all volunteers working with (TMM) of actual or implied liability that may arise now or in the future as a result of the ministry I receive.

I understand that all payments to Healing Hearts and Teia Martinez Ministries are donations. If I cancel an appointment, I can credit my donation to a future appointment. There is a 50% fee for any refunds processed.

Emergency Contact:

Name: _____ Relationship:_____

Number: _____

Signed: _____ Date: _____

Witness: _____ Date: _____

MINOR CONSENT FORM

Please Note: We are a faith-based ministry, and do not charge a fee.

However, we do ask that you prayerfully give a tax-deductible donation for the ministry you receive.

I hereby affirm and state that I am the legal _____ for _____, Date of birth ____/____/____

I hereby consent for _____ to receive personal ministry, the ministry of deliverance, and inner healing that he/she or I/we have requested. I release Teia Martinez Ministries/Healing Hearts International Ministries (TMM/HHIM) and the ministers and deliverance ministry team from any and all liability, actual or implied that may occur as a result of this ministry.

I understand and acknowledge that all ministers, either licensed or lay, that are involved in this ministry are not licensed or trained as psychotherapists, mental health professionals, or professional counselors.

All guidance, counsel, and advice that we receive will be solely based on Scriptural principles and Christian biblical standards as spelled out in the Holy Bible, the written Word of God.

I further understand and acknowledge that all ministry done is solely under the direction and control of the Holy Spirit of God, and that no guarantees are made, nor can be made, with regard to my child's current problem or any future problems.

I understand that all payments to Healing Hearts and Teia Martinez Ministries are donations. If I cancel an appointment, I can credit my donation to a future appointment. There is a 50% fee for any refunds processed.

Emergency Contact:

Name:_____ Relationship:_____ Number:_____

Signed: _____Date: _____

Witnessed: _____Date: _____

VOLUNTEER APPLICATION

Name:_____ Date:_____

Street Address: _____

State:_____ Zip Code: _____ Phone: _____

Email: _____

1)   Briefly state your reasons for wanting to join the Personal Ministry Team.

2)   Briefly describe any experience you have had in the area of personal ministry.

3)   Can you maintain confidential information?   **Yes   No**

4)   Can you commit to volunteer four to five hours per week for ministry?   **Yes   No**

5)   What ministry giftings do you believe you have?
_____ Apostolic _____ Prophetic _____ Evangelist _____ Pastoral _____ Teaching
_____ Counseling_____ Administration _____ Helps _____ Leadership _____ Service
Other: _____

6)   What areas of ministry do you feel called to do?
_____ Deliverance Team/Minister   _____ Personal Ministry Team/Counseling
_____ Administrative/Reception area   _____ Social Media (daily posts & monitoring)
_____ Event Prayer Team   _____ Video recording/editing
_____ Event setup and teardown Team

7)   **When are you available?**
Monday: _____ morning   _____ afternoon _____ evening
Tuesday: _____ morning   _____ afternoon _____ evening
Wednesday: _____ morning   _____ afternoon _____ evening
Thursday: _____ morning   _____ afternoon _____ evening
Friday: _____ morning   _____ afternoon _____ evening
Saturday: _____ morning   _____ afternoon _____ evening

8)   What other ministries are you involved in at this time?

Signature: _____ Date: _____

Please do not write below this line – For Office use only

Notes:

Approved ___   Not Approved ___   Date _____ Initials ___ ___ ___

PERSONAL MINISTRY TEAM – STANDARDS OF CONDUCT AGREEMENT

As a member of the Personal Ministry Team, I agree to the following:
- I will abide by all team standards of conduct.
- I will maintain strict confidentiality for those I have the privilege to minister to. I will not discuss any information that I have access to, either written or spoken, from any source, regarding people being ministered to. I understand this also includes other team members. The only exception is to communicate with the team leader or their Personal Ministry Staff to increase the effectiveness in ministry to the individual.
- I understand that I am committing to being a part of the ministry team schedule, and I am able to be a reliable and consistent part of the team.
- I understand that my granted authority to work in the area of deliverance is confined to ministry approved by the pastoral care department.
- I understand that any deliverance type of ministry on mission trips, street ministry, or other outreaches must be approved by the head of that outreach and are not a part of being on the Personal Ministry Team.
- I agree not to work in the area of deliverance outside of my spiritual covering without formal written approval from the head of the Personal Ministry Team.
- I understand that if I have a breach of confidentiality or fail to abide by the above statements that my status as a Personal Ministry Team member will be revoked and I will no longer be approved to minister.
- I hereby release Teia Martinez and Healing Hearts International Ministries from any and all claims of actual or implied liability that may arise now or in the future from my involvement in this ministry.

By my signature I fully agree with the above statements.

Printed Name: _____

Signature: _____ Date: _____

Personal Ministry Team – Commitment Agreement

We, as deliverance ministers for Teia Martinez Ministries, strive to make a commitment to provide a safe environment to everyone who comes for ministry.

We are committed to confidentiality for each and every person who comes for deliverance. Any discussion/debriefing about a client will be done after sessions with the team leader(s). We agree there will be no discussion outside of the session in any other place or with any other persons.

We also realize the need to come one-half hour before each deliverance session so that we can be prepared to minister at the scheduled time.

Printed Name: _____

Signature: _____ Date: _____

WALKING OUT YOUR FREEDOM

Deliverance is the beginning of your freedom, not the end. We receive deliverance from past hurts, wounds, and bondages, and then we press on toward the goal. No matter where we come from or where we have been, we have a new citizenship. We are a new creation. We are no longer of this world; our citizenship is in Heaven and we are here to bring God's Kingdom "on earth as it is in Heaven." Knowing this will help us to keep our focus on the goal. Also know that the enemy will not give up. There will still be temptations, trials, tests, and attacks. When we are under attack, we need to know, "This too will pass." Everything in this life is temporary.

In walking out deliverance, it is helpful to know a couple of Scriptures. Matthew 12:43-45, "When an evil spirit comes out of a man, it goes through arid places seeking rest and does not find it. Then it says, 'I will return to the house I left.' When it arrives, it finds the house unoccupied, swept clean, and put in order. Then it goes and takes with it seven other spirits more wicked than itself, and they go in and live there. And the final condition of that man is worse than the first. That is how it will be with this wicked generation." We want to make sure that, if and when that spirit returns, he finds that house full of the Holy Spirit and the power of God! To do this, we must be baptized in the Holy Spirit and we must be full of the Word of God.

The next Scripture is John 5:1-15, the story of the man at the pool of Bethesda. In verse 8, Jesus said to him, "Get up! Pick up your mat and walk." and the man was instantly cured. Following in verse 14 it says, "Later Jesus found him at the temple and said to him, 'See, you are well again. Stop sinning or something worse may happen to you.'" Most bondage comes in through sin, and most spirits and strongholds are fed by sin. To walk out our deliverance and to stay free, we too should go and sin no more!

We also need to be people of forgiveness, letting no root of bitterness spring up in us. Hebrews 12:14 says, "pursue peace with all people." Also, we should change old habits. Sin, as well as bad habits, open the door for the devil to put hooks in us. We need to ask God to show us any bad habits we have and how to break them. To walk in freedom, we must walk in the truth of the Word of God and not by feelings. Feelings are up and down, and if we walk by our feelings, we too will be up and down. We are called to walk by faith, and in the Spirit - then we will walk in Freedom! Revelation 12:11 says, "We are overcomers by the Blood of the Lamb and the word of our testimony." Our testimony reminds us of where we came from and what God has delivered us from. There is power in your story with God!

Hopefully, you will have learned to do this during your deliverance, but make sure your home is clean of anything from the past. Ask the Holy Spirit to guide you. Get rid of ungodly music, movies/tv shows, books, pictures, magazines, letters, photos, knick-knacks, idols, witchcraft items, Masonic items and jewelry, and of course any articles of affection from an affair or ungodly relationship. If you ask the Holy Spirit, He will guide you, and if you are in doubt - get rid of it. The person who has been set free will want to do this, to be free in every area of life.

If you have never been water baptized, you need to be. Jesus was water baptized. What greater example could we have, to know this is a powerful thing for our lives? We encourage you to ask the Lord to show you what He wants to show you during this time. Statistically most new Christians who backslide were never baptized. Baptism is a command, not an option.

The next thing is getting connected with other believers at a church or ministry gathering, and becoming accountable to someone: a small group leader, a pastor, a mature brother or sister in the Lord. Get connected and start serving other people. Finally, do not wait for the enemy to attack; the best defense is a good offense. Get into the Word, pray every day, put on the full armor of God according to Ephesians chapter 6, and advance the Kingdom of God. Get to know Him personally. Witness, testify, walk and talk Jesus, and above all else, guard your thoughts. You are what you think! Know that the battlefield is your mind. Take authority over it, walk in freedom, and stay free!

CONFESSIONS FOR OVERCOMERS

Proverbs 18:21 says, "The tongue has the power of life and death..." Our words are powerful! To receive the full power of these Scriptures, pray them out loud every day for 40 days.. you can also put them on your walls mirrors anywhere you can see throughout the day. Everything in the world speaks to us. Signs when we drive, music, tv, social media, it is important to have God's word speaking to you every day, throughout your day. These prayers are powerful because of the authority of the Holy Spirit in you. When we profess the Word, it gets the Word deep into us. The things the enemy says are then no longer familiar, they become foreign, and the Truth reigns in your mind. Renewing the mind has the old way of thinking and the old man die, and allows the new man, the new creation, to be born again. It is vital that we renew the mind. It affects our heart, our tongue, and our choices.

Ask the Holy Spirit to give you revelation on each truth, each Scripture!

I am a child of God, adopted into His family through Jesus Christ (Ephesians 1:5).

I am God's masterpiece, created in Christ Jesus to do good works (Ephesians 2:10).

I am the righteousness of God in Christ, made new through His sacrifice (2 Corinthians 5:21).

I am a chosen people, a royal priesthood, a holy nation, God's special possession (1 Peter 2:9).

I am a temple of the Holy Spirit; God's Spirit lives in me (1 Corinthians 3:16).

I am more than a conqueror through Him who loves me (Romans 8:37).

No weapon formed against me shall prosper, and every tongue that rises against me in judgment I shall condemn (Isaiah 54:17).

Greater is He who is in me than he who is in the world (1 John 4:4).

I am strong and courageous; I will not be afraid or discouraged because the Lord my God is with me wherever I go (Joshua 1:9).

I can do all things through Christ who strengthens me (Philippians 4:13).

The Lord fights for me, and I hold my peace (Exodus 14:14).

God has not given me a spirit of fear, but of power, love, and a sound mind (2 Timothy 1:7).

MINISTRY PROCESS STEPS

Intake

- Client makes initial contact, via phone or email

- Our office emails appropriate questionnaire and consent form

- Client sends forms back prior to their initial appointment

- We review the forms, assess where they need deliverance or inner healing work by looking at paperwork

Inner Healing

- Client has regular weekly appointments with their minister

- Forgiveness homework, Generational Curses, and Freemasonry are done with every client prior to Deliverance

- Other prayers as needed, led by Holy Spirit

- Inner Healing for trauma/memory healing

- Number of appointments can vary widely, from 3-4, all the way to 6+ months until the client and minister feels they are ready for deliverance

Deliverance

- Client goes through deliverance with a team, in either 3, 2-hour sessions, or a 2 day intensive

- Deliverance Prayer is prayed by client before each session

- Team takes client through 16 strongholds, broken up between sessions

- Bless and fill client back up following each session

- Sealing Prayer to end each session

Follow-Up

- Follow-up paperwork is given to walk out healing

- Client is able to schedule additional inner healing/ministry appointments as needed, often every 6 mos-1 year

ABOUT THE AUTHOR

Teia Martinez is the founder of Teia Martinez Ministries and the Inner Healing and Deliverance office, Healing Hearts International Ministries, established in 2017. With a heart for revival, Teia leads a dedicated team of ministers and volunteers who help others experience freedom, healing, and breakthrough. Thousands have encountered transformation through her ministry, which she and her husband, Carlos, relocated to the Houston, Texas area in 2021. Together, they have three grown children, and five grandchildren. This is Teia's second book, following Deliverance and Inner Healing for Children and Teens.

Facebook
www.facebook.com/TeiaMartinezMinistries

Website
www.teiamartinezministries.com

TEIA MARTINEZ
MINISTRIES

If your life has been
touched by the power
of God through this
ministry...

BECOME A MONTHLY PARTNER FOR FREEDOM!

Your participation as a monthly supporter
relieves us of the burden of meeting our
overhead of rent, utilities and other office costs,
and enables us to wholly concentrate on the
tasks that God has given us.

We believe there is much work to do so that the
body of Christ can be healed and fully
equipped. Your gift will enable us to continue to
minister to those in need of healing, training,
and discipleship. We send a regular email
newsletter with testimonies and information on
all activities within the ministry.

HEAD TO OUR WEBSITE AND CLICK "PARTNER" TO JOIN US!

teiamartinezministries.com

Association of
FRONTLINE GENERALS

GET EQUIPPED FOR YOUR DESTINY!

LICENSURE AND ORDINATION FOR MINISTERS

THE GOAL OF THE ASSOCIATION OF FRONTLINE GENERALS IS
TO MENTOR, TRAIN, ESTABLISH AND MULTIPLY
RELATIONSHIPS THAT SEE THE KINGDOM OF GOD GROW IN
POWER AND AUTHORITY.

For more information:
teiamartinezministries.com/frontline-generals

ASSOCIATION OF
FRONTLINE
GENERALS

Inner Healing & Deliverance for Children & Teens

Visit our website for more information!

teiamartinezministries.com

A Practical Guide for Deliverance to Children

By Teia Martinez